BIBLIOGRAPHIC
INSTRUCTION
AND THE
LEARNING
PROCESS

LIBRARY ORIENTATION SERIES

BIBLIOGRAPHIC INSTRUCTION AND THE LEARNING PROCESS:

THEORY, STYLE AND MOTIVATION

Papers Presented at the Twelfth Annual
Library Instruction Conference
held at Eastern Michigan University, May 6 & 7, 1982

edited by
Carolyn A. Kirkendall
Director, Project LOEX
Center of Educational Resources
Eastern Michigan University

Published for the
Center of Educational Resources,
Eastern Michigan University
by

Pierian Press
ANN ARBOR, MICHIGAN
1984

14486

Library of Congress Catalog Card No. 84-60638
ISBN 0-87650-182-X

PIERIAN PRESS
P.O. Box 1808
Ann Arbor, Michigan 48106

Contents

Preface

Carolyn A. Kirkendall
Director
LOEX Clearinghouse

The Twelfth Annual Library Instruction Conference was held on May 6 & 7, 1982, at Eastern Michigan University. Sponsored by the national LOEX Library Instruction Clearinghouse, this meeting, as its immediate predecessor, reflected an emphasis on the broader range of library instruction activity on the college and university levels rather than earlier interest in library orientation as a major focus.

The printed presentations are included in the order they were presented, to maintain the essential flavor and format of the meeting. Editing of remarks has been intentionally limited. It is tempting at times to reword presentations to provide a more homogenous reading style, but I've opted to allow each speaker to appear in print in his/her own words. Also, as in the past, readers are reminded that speakers for this Conference were originally invited to address the broad theme of the meeting. This year's topic was "Library Instruction and Learning: Theories, Styles, and Motivations." Each speaker was requested to address the topic in a general manner, but it is sometimes chancy to assume that all presentors will do so in an obvious fashion, and on occasion conference preceedings may deviate somewhat from the main theme.

While isolated presentations concerned with bibliographic instruction and learning theory had been given in the past, this Conference represents the first time that the specific topic was exclusively addressed. A reading list (included in this volume) was compiled and provided to each Conference participant beforehand, so that the audience would be prepared with background knowledge on the topic. Ellison's article in *Catholic Library World* contains the most basic and helpful discussion of how the learning process and bibliographic instruction are related.

vii

The importance of applying learning theories to instruction in library use was introduced by the keynote speaker, Cerise Oberman. Aluri and Reichel delineated these theories, while Freimer and Wallace provided a summary version of a model they are currently preparing. Motivation as a factor in the learning process was explored by Morell Boone. Specific library user groups, including foreign students, were targeted by Wayman, Brock and King. Mellon provided a description of her local library instruction experience to emphasize the essential role of faculty support to a program solidly based on instructional design and learning theory. As it is always interesting to compare how library learners are instructed in other countries, a description by Megan Lilly from Australia was included in the program as was a summary of how British user education programs differ from our own, this from Connie Mulligan from Kentucky. Lindgren presented a unique discussion of the basic learning processes of reasoning, writing and research as they apply to library use instruction.

Sponsoring this Conference each year continues to be a remarkably enjoyable task. Participants seem to arrive in Ypsilanti eager to listen and discuss, reticent to challenge and criticize. Attendance continues to average about one-half first-timers, about one-half repeaters. Helping to make this particular Conference a successful experience were Sue Parks, the LOEX secretary, staff at the EMU Division of Continuing Education and the McKenny Union, Hannelore B. Rader, who so loyally prepares our annual BI bibliography, and Oak Woods Media, Neal-Schuman and Pierian Press, publishers who continue to provide their generous support in sponsoring our annual Conference parties. And special thanks go, of course, to our talented and knowledgeable speakers, who were responsible for providing us with a comprehensive and lively description of the library instruction/learning connection.

WHY THEORY?
OR THE END OF BIBLIOGRAPHIC INSTRUCTION

Cerise Oberman
University of Minnesota

While attending ALA Mid-winter in Denver this past January, usually a busy, but generally uneventful occurrence, I happened into a conversation which has remained with me long after the snow-capped mountain peaks of the Rockies melted from my memory. As you might expect, the conversation was centered on bibliographic instruction. I had shown the manuscript I was working on for a book of collected essays on theories being used in bibliographic instruction to a colleague. I was feeling pretty good about the manuscript and, perhaps, a bit smug in knowing that this was the first attempt to gather together this information. After all, it had been apparent to those in the heart of instruction, that the word "theory" had become the new catchword for instruction librarians. Papers, workshops, articles, pre-conferences, and conferences have focused on theory. Obviously, the need was there. I, myself, felt it.

Perhaps within that context, you can imagine my shock when my colleague, who had just finished browsing the manuscript, looked straight into my eyes and asked, "Why do we need theory in our instruction programs?" I was dumbfounded. His own involvement in bibliographic instruction is well-known and highly regarded; that made me all the more incredulous. Why should he even raise the issue, when I had so fully taken it for granted? My respect for him, however, made me listen. He continued, making the argument that, for the most part, instruction in how to use a library was effectively being designed, taught, and positively accepted. What could be more straightforward than teaching the card catalog? Or how to analyze an index? Why overlap the obvious with the esoteric? Why confuse the issues and make them more complex than they need be?

Since January, I have given that conversation a good deal of thought. His case is quite convincing; the position well taken. If we look at the instructional objectives of the ACRL BI Task Force, they clearly state that the "Primary role of bibliographic instruction

1

is to provide students with the specific skills needed to successfully complete their assignments."[1] Most of us, I believe, are accomplishing that objective with relative assurance. Yet here we are at a conference whose theme is theory not skills. This seems to indicate that we are responding to one of two things.

Perhaps we are responding to an advertisement. In other words, we are simply reacting to a need that has been created, rather than one that actually exists. How often do we flip on the television only to be barraged by advertisements for products that will correct problems that we never knew we had? Did we ever really worry about "ring-around-the-collar," or room odors, or sexy teeth before we were told we should? Likewise, is the concept of theory in bibliographic instruction a product we simply do not need, but are being sold?

Or is it possible that the natural evolution of bibliographic instruction has brought us to our present posture — a point which recognizes that bibliographic instruction, although successful, is in a stage of arrested methodological development. In other words, is theory the next logical step in the growth and development of bibliographic instruction?

It is my contention that the latter is the case. Bibliographic instruction is in the midst of exploring and expanding its theoretical foundations as part of a continuing spectrum of growth. The current obsession with theory is a natural and predictable occurrence if we consider bibliographic instruction a developing discipline.

The notion of bibliographic instruction as an emerging entity in its own right is not a new one. Two years ago, Fran Hopkins presented a perceptive and prophetic analysis of the state of bibliographic instruction.[2] At that time, she made a convincing argument that instruction librarians were emerging as a splinter group or subspecialty within librarianship. She went as far as suggesting that instruction librarians had more "in common with an academic discipline than with traditional librarianship."[3] Hopkins based her conclusion on several factors: common personality traits found in instruction librarians; allotment and organization of time that instruction librarians spent in the development, deliverance, and administration of instruction programs; and, perhaps most importantly, the search for the theoretical missing link. When that missing link was discovered, when instruction librarians established a theoretical basis for their work, Hopkins concluded, then they would indeed emerge as separatists.

I remember quite clearly that the LOEX audience that year received her remarks with great enthusiasm. Yet, I had reservations about library instruction pronouncing itself a separate discipline. I had two concerns. First, I worried what implications such an

2

announcement would have on academic librarianship in general. Second, I did not know if bibliographic instruction could really define itself as a discipline.

Today, for a number of reasons, I fear less the consequences of bibliographic instruction announcing its separation. At the same time, however, I have also been convinced that library instruction is emerging, if not as a totally separate discipline, then at least as a distinct sub-specialty which may ultimately be viewed as a branch of librarianship.

My own work in searching for that theoretical missing link in bibliographic instruction has led me to this point. Although my own research has centered on cognitive theory and its practical application, I have spent the last two years trying to document the variety of theory now being used in bibliographic instruction programs. When I was examining the theoretical basis which one of our colleagues proposed for use in teaching library instruction, Fran Hopkins' words sprang to mind. In searching for justification for including theory in bibliographic instruction, Michael Keresteszi's theoretical foundation for bibliographic instruction becomes particularly useful.

Michael Keresteszi's theory is an analysis of the systematic development of disciplines. It is his system which I will use to examine the growth and emergence of bibliographic instruction. Furthermore, it is his system which we can use as a yardstick to measure how far bibliographic instruction has progressed in establishing itself as a sub-specialty. Finally, it is his system which will help shed some light on the question of "why bother with theory in bibliographic instruction now?"

II

Keresteszi identifies three distinct stages in the development of an academic discipline: the pioneering stage; the elaboration and proliferation stage; and the establishment stage. His basic premise is that all emerging disciplines pass through these three stages; the rate of movement from one stage of development to the next, however, may vary greatly. A generalized model of discipline development is possible, Keresteszi asserts, because all disciplines, regardless of their subject content, are "marked by certain characteristics in the epistemological orientation, methodological concerns, the social and organizational makeup, modes of communication, and the forms and quantity of literature produced."[4] In other words, all disciplines share many of the same characteristics in establishing themselves as separate entities. Likewise they produce much of the same types of literature to document this separation.

3

Thus, Keresteszi plots discipline development by tracing major events or developments in the emergence of a discipline and the corresponding reaction to that event or development. That reaction takes the form of a type of communication, (i.e., written or oral) and/or a bibliographic response, (i.e., materials, books, journals, etc.).

Comparing the growth of bibliographic instruction with Keresteszi's structural development pattern proves quite illuminating. The past and the present growth of bibliographic instruction seem to parallel his model extensively. (If there is a validity to this consequence, Keresteszi may also have much to tell us about our future.)

The Pioneering Stage in a discipline's development is marked by its struggle for recognition. In this early stage, a new idea or concept is conceived and then spread by various modes of communication. Library instruction seems to have successfully completed all the steps which constitute the Pioneering Stage.

Keresteszi charts the specific events and modes of communication in the development of a discipline; the growth of bibliographic instruction falls neatly into place in his paradigm.

The Pioneering Stage[5]

Events/development

1. The great thinker, or prophet emerges.

Modes of communication/bibliographic response

1. Individual contacts, and use of a number of accessible channels to communicate new discoveries are used.

Bibliographic instruction has its ideological roots in the 19th-century,[6] but the current instruction movement owes its ideological roots to a number of contemporary visionaries, and perhaps, most of all, to Patricia Knapp. In any event, these visionaries, many of whom are still active in instruction today, began an informal communications network.

2. Groups of dissidents branch off from the mainstream.

2. Characterized by the establishment of special panels.

As early as 1967, ALA established the Instruction in the Use of Libraries Committee to promote and coordinate instruction activity in ALA units.

4

3. Efforts to propagandize; convert.   3. Abundance of fugitive materials, circulars, etc.

In the early years, instruction librarians were often spoken of as evangelical. Indeed, by 1972, the interest in library instruction had swollen to such proportions that over 2,000 librarians attended a multi-media show of library instruction materials at the 1972 ALA conference.[7]

4. Small band of followers group together who know one another personally.   4. An invisible college emerges.

No one would call the 2,000 librarians who attended the multi-media show a small band of followers, but those few librarians who were innovators at this time really did form a small invisible college. In the next stage of development this invisible college becomes more formalized.

5. Efforts to keep in touch and maintain ideological cohesion.   5. Bulletins and newsletters.

In 1972, Project LOEX was established to serve as both a depository and distributor for information and material on instructional activities. Its newsletter has served as a mechanism for informing instruction librarians of current trends and publications in bibliographic instruction.

6. Attempts to gain legitimacy.   6. Followers place articles in established journals, publish books, present papers at conferences and seminars.

From 1973 to 1979 there was a 472 percent increase in published English language material on bibliographic instruction.[8]

7. Financing through own efforts.   7. Grant proposals, annual reports to the sponsors.

The Council on Library Resources offered three separate grant programs for library instruction. From 1969 until recently, grants were awarded and annual reports submitted.[9] In addition, grants were available to library instruction projects from other federal grant programs (i.e., National Science Foundation) as well as private sources.

    The characteristics of the Pioneering Stage are attention, converts, and recognition. It is self-evident that bibliographic instruction as an idea struggled for attention and received it, sought converts and made them, fought for recognition and won it.

Bibliographic instruction is now firmly entrenched in the second stage of Keresteszi's discipline development — the Elaboration and Proliferation Stage. This stage is characterized by the continued proliferation of ideas through publication and conferences. But, it is also marked by a gradual, but significant shift in the content of material. According to Keresteszi, "while earlier works were either topical or problem-specific, now there is [an] excessive preoccupation with methodology."[10] Let us examine the steps of this stage which brings us to the important turning point in a discipline's development, the point at which bibliographic instruction is presently.

The Elaboration and Proliferation Stage

Events/developments

1. Followers multiply, spread all over the world.

2. Practitioners of discipline no longer all know one another personally.

Modes of communication/bibliographic responses

1. Membership roster and directories.

I view these first two developments as one. Indeed, the idea of bibliographic instruction has spread like wildfire. Foreign interest ranges from Great Britain to South Africa, from Sweden to Australia. In the last few years LOEX has given us an opportunity to hear a number of our foreign colleagues; this conference will be no exception. The production of directories, however, has remained localized; directories of state and regional library instruction programs have taken precedence over national or international directories.[11] Perhaps a larger scale directory is in our future.

3. Interaction among the people in the field becomes structured and formalized.

3. National association formed; committees, conferences, symposia, published proceedings, papers, reports, studies, yearbooks, official journal.

We have accomplished this step so well that there is too much to explore within the scope of this paper. So, a few highlights. National association: while there is no national association solely dedicated to instruction, the creation of the Bibliographic Instruction Section within the ACRL section of ALA and the creation of LIRT (Library Instruction Roundtable), also in ALA, stand as the core organizations for instruction librarians. Committees: In ACRL BIS, the committee structure has been very productive in producing standards and recommendations for instruction librarians on a wide range of subjects. Conferences: in 1979 alone there were thirty-two known conferences or workshops held on bibliographic instruction.[12] Published Proceedings: both national conferences held in 1979 published their proceedings.[13] Official journal: last year the ACRL BIS Think Tank issued a report which recommended that the bibliographic instruction movement have its own journal.[14] I am delighted to announce that such a journal will make its debut, under the able leadership of Sharon Hogan and Mary George, this fall. The title: *Research Strategies: A Journal of Library Concepts & Instruction.*

4. Concern for training of future practitioners.	4. Standards or guides; textbooks and manuals.

There have been a number of books and manuals on bibliographic instruction, some geared to the practitioner, others, more recently, geared to the library school student. In addition, the ACRL BIS Committee on Education for Bibliographic Instruction has been actively working to encourage inclusion of graduate course offerings in library instruction.

5. Subject matter becomes more and more complicated, discipline breaks up into subfields; preoccupation with methodology.	5. New invisible colleges; new modes of research; separate journals with narrower focus.

This is the last step which I will discuss, although there are nine more steps which comprise this stage of development. But this is the step at which I think we currently find ourselves.

Since the rejuvenation of the instruction movement in the 1960s, the subject matter has become more diversified. The main themes which have emerged are program development; instructional material preparation; program evaluation; and program administration. For the most part, these topics have concentrated on the practical and tangible aspects of library instruction. But recently, there has been an uneasiness, a restlessness, about the limited scope of instruction literature. This restlessness may stem, as Hopkins suggests in her paper, from the lack of consensus on the mission of instruction librarians.[15] Sometimes it feels as if we are going in all directions, yet missing the most important one. The time has arrived, as Arthur Young suggests in a recent review of instruction literature, when "conceptual clarification is needed to transcend the artificial dichotomy of instruction or information."[16] New modes of research centering around theory are emerging. Correspondingly, an invisible college of persons involved in theory also formed. The general movement is underway.

At ALA's National Conference in New York in 1980, over three hundred librarians turned out for an ACRL program which promised to begin making that transcendence. A year later, ACRL BIS hosted a pre-conference; two workshops out of six concentrated on concepts or theories for teaching. And this year ACRL's program in Philadelphia will once again address this question.[17] And of course, over 150 people are gathered here, eager to learn about the place of theory in bibliographic instruction.

The emergence of theory as a dominant theme at this time is not accidental. It is necessary, and possibly even inevitable, if bibliographic instruction is following a course of discipline development. Contrary to the popular belief of a few years ago that bibliographic instruction was resting on a plateau,[18] I see it ascending a mountain. And at the summit is recognition, both implicit and explicit, of bibliographic instruction as a specialty.

III

If we have satisfactorily answered the question of why theory seems to be predominating bibliographic instruction at this juncture, there still remains another basic question: what exactly is bibliographic instruction theory? Or perhaps, is there *a* theory of or for bibliographic instruction? There are no single or simple answers to these questions. In fact, it is the diversity of answers which makes this time in bibliographic instruction so exciting.

It is not within the scope of this paper to summarize the many specific theories which are emerging. Mary Reichel and Rao Aluri will, I am sure, cover some of these in depth. Instead, I would like to briefly examine what I consider the major trends that theoretical approaches are taking. I see two primary directions of theoretical formulation and application: the "inside" approach and the "outside" approach.

The "inside" approach has turned to the very heart of librarianship — information and information structure — to begin building a theoretical base for library instruction. The "inside" theories are characterized by their emphasis on one or more of the following:

the structure of bibliographic information; the correspondence which exists between substantive and bibliographic information; citation indexing structures; the structure of discipline research; and the development of disciplines.[19]

The impetus for this approach is well expressed by two of our colleagues who are actively plotting out and applying these theories to bibliographic instruction. Topsy Smalley and Stephen Plum are concentrating on "driving the center of concern back . . . to a framework of concepts about the structures of the disciplines and their research process. These contexts," they contend, "generate the distinctive qualities of information systems and strategies for bibliographic inquiry."[20] In other words, by examining the structures of the disciplines and how scholars in those disciplines pursue research, we are exposing the unique search strategies which can be used as the basis for teaching bibliographic instruction.

By examining the structure of knowledge and information systems, we are laying the groundwork, the foundation, for librarians to transcend disciplines. We are also providing the most essential concept to our students — an understanding of models and concepts of information generation and structure. According to Michael Keresteszi, we also are finding our own niche within the academic world. To bridge the distance between scholars and librarians, Keresteszi urges librarians to "seek the solution [not] in the acquisition of degrees in practice-oriented subject disciplines, but [rather] by preserving proudly our generalist posture, we should cultivate our own garden."[21] This approach to bibliographic instruction does just that.

The "outside" group has turned its attention beyond the immediate scope of traditional librarianship; they have turned to education and psychology. This group has been predominantly interested in applying learning theory to already existing bibliographic instruction programs or, more recently, developing instruction programs based upon learning theory.

Bruner, Ausubel, Gagne, Dewey, Piaget, Skinner — most of us never heard these names in library school, yet now they seem to be appearing everywhere. The work of these psychologists and educational philosophers has contributed greatly to understanding the process of intellectual development, problem-solving, and transference of knowledge.

By examining these various concepts of learning, the "outside" group is developing a basic understanding of the foundation of learning. This foundation will be the basis for the preparation of programs, presentations, and materials. This foundation will speak directly to educating, rather than to instructing. The form or format of instruction is often dictated by a particular learning theory. Emphasis on the model of instruction, e.g., workbooks, guided design, computer-assisted instruction, is less important, however, than the underlying theory which dictates its content.[22]

Through an understanding of how students learn, both behaviorally and cognitively, the "outside" group is examining not only its methodologies, but the very essence of the content of library instruction. In other words, like the "inside" group, the "outside" group is changing the substance of bibliographic instruction as a result of this new dimension. Emphasis is placed on analyzing information needs, evaluating resources, and using evidence as a basis of inquiry. Process is supreme.

The "inside" and "outside" groups at first glance seem to be moving in opposite directions: the "inside" group concentrating on foundations of knowledge and theories of bibliography, while the "outside" group pursues application of learning theories. But the groups have something essential in common: each of the groups is reassessing the basis of present teaching approaches. Each is changing not only the form but the content of bibliographic instruction. For the first time, library instruction has begun to isolate substantive concepts to teach our students, and present those concepts in designs which will facilitate their understanding and application.

As both the "inside" and the "outside" groups become more stabilized, interweaving of their theories and their approaches will further clarify the "muddy goals of library instruction" which Fran Hopkins spoke of two years ago.[23] Moreover, as research continues, bibliographic instruction as we have known it in the past ten years will undergo further transformation: it will distinguish itself further as a separate entity, and perhaps even subsume the reference function completely.[24]

IV

Today, I feel a little less dumbfounded than I did in Denver. And perhaps I have Mid-winter and my colleague to thank for helping me sort out the question of the role of theory in bibliographic instruction. Now, I think, I have an answer to give him. Theoretical foundations provide bibliographic instruction with options, options to finally and forever leave behind the characterization of bibliographic instruction as simply mechanical. It is time to abandon instruction altogether as a rubric for the teaching that librarians do. Instruction, though seen as successful, is only one-dimensional, implying the imparting of specific skills. Theory, on the other hand, allows us the freedom of adopting education as our purpose and our goal. Education denotes long range planning and meaning; education includes instruction but encompasses so much more. Education means a concern with the relation of any subject matter to all other subject

10

matters and possibly even to life-long needs. Instruction has only been part of our mission — education is now the rest.

Notes

1. Association of College and Research Libraries. Bibliographic Task Force. "Guidelines for Bibliographic Instruction in Academic Libraries," *College & Research Libraries News* 38 (April 1977): 92. A revised statement of objectives appears in Association of College and Research Libraries. Bibliographic Instruction Section. Policy and Planning Committee. *Bibliographic Instruction Handbook*. (Chicago: ACRL, 1979.)

2. Frances L. Hopkins, "Bibliographic Instruction: An Emerging Professional Discipline," in *Directions for the Decade: Library Instruction in the 1980s*, ed. Carolyn A. Kirkendall (Ann Arbor, MI: Pierian Press, 1981), pp. 13–24.

3. Ibid., p13.

4. Michael Keresteszi, "The Science of Bibliography: Theoretical Implications for Bibliographic Instruction," in *Theories of Bibliographic Education: Design for Teaching*, eds. Cerise Oberman and Katina Strauch (New York: Bowker, 1982), p13.

5. Both the Pioneering Stage and the Elaboration and Proliferation Stage models are reproduced by permission of Michael Keresteszi. For the concluding steps of the Elaboration and Proliferation Stage and the entire Establishment Stage see: Ibid., p16–17, 19.

6. John Mark Tucker, "User Education in Academic Libraries: A Century in Retrospect," *Library Trends* 29 (Summer 1980): 10–12.

7. Sharon Anne Hogan, "Training and Education of Library Instruction Librarians," *Library Trends* 29 (Summer 1980): 107.

8. This figure was determined by comparing the statistics on English language publications recorded by Hannelore B. Rader in her annual bibliographies on library instruction which appear in *Reference Services Review*.

9. See Nancy E. Gwinn, "Academic Libraries and Undergraduate Education. The CLR Experience," *College and Research Libraries*

41 (June 1980): p5–16 for a review of CLR programs and reports.

10. Keresteszi, "Science of Bibliography," p15.

11. A list of directories appears in American Library Association, Association of College and Research Libraries. Bibliographic Instruction Section, Committee on Cooperation, Clearinghouse Subcommittee, "Library Instruction Clearinghouse: Depositories and Publications, 1980."

12. See Hogan, "Training and Education," p124--126 for a complete list of conferences held in 1979.

13. *Proceedings from the 2nd Southeastern Conference on Approaches to Bibliographic Instruction, March 22--23, 1979*, ed. Cerise Oberman-Soroka (Charleston, SC: College of Charleston Library Associates, 1980) and *Reform and Renewal in Higher Education: Implications for Library Instruction* (Library Orientation Series, no. 10) ed. Carolyn A. Kirkendall (Ann Arbor, MI: Pierian Press, 1980).

14. "Think Tank Recommendations for Bibliographic Instruction," *College and Research Libraries News* 42 (December 1981): 397.

15. Hopkins, "Bibliographic Instruction," p16.

16. Arthur P. Young, "And Gladly Teach: Bibliographic Instruction and the Library," *Advances in Librarianship* 10 (1980): 80.

17. ALA New York, 1980: ACRL Bibliographic Instruction Section, "Learning Theory in Action: Applications in Bibliographic Instruction," speakers: Sharon J. Rogers, "Theoretical Designs: Issues, Questions, Procedures" and Cerise Oberman-Soroka, "Petals Around a Rose: Abstract Reasoning and Bibliographic Instruction," July 1, 1980. ALA San Francisco, 1981: ACRL Bibliographic Instruction Section, "Premises, Problems, Promises: Views and Approaches to Bibliographic Instruction." Workshops on Theory: Mary Reichel, Mary Ann Ramey, Gemma DeVinney, "Conceptual Frameworks for Bibliographic Instruction Presentations," and Cerise Oberman-Soroka and Mark Schlesinger, "Cognitive Learning in Bibliographic Instruction," June 24–26, 1981. ALA Philadelphia, 1982: ACRL Bibliographic Instruction Section, "Back to the Books: Bibliographic Instruction and the Theory of Information Sources," Speakers:

Patrick Wilson, Frances L. Hopkins, Conrad H. Rawski, Thomas Kirk.

18. See "Library Instruction: A Column of Opinion," ed. Carolyn Kirkendall, *Journal of Academic Librarianship* 5 (November 1979): 284–285 for a discussion of this issue.

19. A number of "inside" theories are documented in essays by Topsy Smalley and Stephen Plum; Michael Keresteszi; and Raymond McInnis appearing in *Theories in Bibliographic Education: Designs for Teaching*.

20. Topsy N. Smalley and Stephen H. Plum, "Teaching Library Researching in the Humanities and the Sciences: A Conceptual Approach," in *Theories in Bibliographic Education: Designs for Teaching*, p137.

21. Keresteszi, "Science of Bibliography," p26.

22. For examples of applications of learning theory to instruction programs see essays by Jon Lindgren; Constance A. Mellon; Patricia A. Berge and Judith Pryor; Cerise Oberman and Rebecca Linton; Mitsuko Williams and Elisabeth B. Davis; and Elizabeth Frick in *Theories for Bibliographic Education: Designs for Teaching*.

23. For an excellent example of the interweaving of learning theory and foundations of knowledge see Smalley and Plum, "Teaching Library Researching."

24. The ACRL Think Tank Report touched upon this issue when it recommended that bibliographic instruction should be "viewed . . . as the very heart of the reference process." Raymond G. McInnis, in his *New Perspective for Reference Service in Academic Libraries* (Contributions in Librarianship and Information Science, 23). Westport, CT: Greenwood Press, 1978, also implicitly suggests this shift.

LEARNING THEORIES
AND BIBLIOGRAPHIC INSTRUCTION

Rao Aluri
Emory University
and
Mary Reichel
Georgia State University

Introduction

This presentation is divided into two sections: the first section surveys behavioral and cognitive learning theories[1] and the second section deals with the application of these theories to bibliographic instruction.

I. Learning Theories

Learning is defined as "a relatively permanent change in behavior or knowledge brought about by practice or experience."[2] The emphasis of learning theories, then, is to discover how experience or practice affects learner behavior. Currently, there are two dominant theories of learning: Behavioral (or conditioning) and Cognitive theories. These theories explain how learning takes place from two different perspectives. In the next few minutes we will see how these two theories differ in their assumptions and explanations of how learning takes place. First, we will deal with behavioral theory followed by cognitive perspective.

IA. Behavioral Theory of Learning

Behavioral theory of learning has its origins in the works of empiricist philosophers such as Locke, Hobbs, Berkeley, Hume, and the Mills. The fundamental beliefs behind this theory are: (1) all knowledge is derived from sensory experience, (2) all knowledge or ideas can be broken down into simpler basic units, (3) ideas are formed by the association of experiences occurring closely together in time, and (4) it is not necessary to assume that the mind has complex and mysterious structures, instead, it is sufficient to assume that the mind is a blank slate on which new experiences are recorded and stored.[3] Starting from these assumptions, Watson, Thorndike, Hull,

Guthrie, and Skinner built and elaborated upon the behavioristic view of learning. Behaviorists emphasize observable phenomena and deemphasize mental structures and introspection. Learning takes place, according to this view, only when overt, observable behavioral change takes place.

Behaviorism explains two types of learning — involuntary and purposeful learnings. Classical conditioning, pioneered by Pavlov, explains the involuntary learning and Skinner's operant (or instrumental) conditioning seeks to explain the goal seeking behavior. Classical conditioning is based on the existence of involuntary reflexes where the presence of a stimulus elicits a response from an organism. For example, the presence of a food elicits salivation in a dog. In this case, food is an unconditioned stimulus and salivation is an unconditioned response. Classical conditioning makes use of these preexisting reflexes in that an organism is presented with a stimulus to be learned in conjunction with a reinforcing unconditioned stimulus. For instance, to teach a dog to salivate whenever a bell is rung, the dog is presented the conditioning stimulus of the ringing bell and the unconditioned stimulus of food together repeatedly. After some time, the dog learns to salivate when the conditioned stimulus (ringing bell) alone is presented. In this example, the ringing bell is the learning material and the food acts as a reinforcement for learning. In any case, the conditioning perspective views the learning as the development and strengthening of stimulus-response (S-R) bonds.

In the classical conditioning environment, the learner is passive as a stimulus must exist for the learner to respond. Skinner's operant conditioning theory attempts to account for situations where the response is initiated by the learner although no recognizable stimulus exists. In both classical and operant conditioning, the unconditioned stimulus acts as a reinforcement for learning. However, classical and operant conditioning theories differ in two respects — one, in terms of the *sequence* of stimuli and responses and, two, in terms of *responses* made by the learner. In terms of sequence of events, in classical conditioning, both conditioned and unconditioned stimuli *precede* the response while in operant conditioning, the response *precedes* the stimulus or reinforcement. In terms of the type of response, classical conditioning best explains the learner's involuntary responses such as salivation and emotional responses such as fear and anxiety. Both these types of responses are controlled by the learner's autonomous nervous system. Operant conditioning, on the other hand, is related to the learner's voluntary skeletal and muscular reactions. In other words, in classical conditioning, the learner *responds* to the stimulus whereas in operant conditioning the learner *operates* on his/her environment.[4]

Despite these differences, both conditioning perspectives explain a number of features of learning.[5] Both theories emphasize that the material to be learned and the corresponding reinforcement must occur together in time for learning to take place. Learning can be reinforced by repeatedly presenting the learning material and the reinforcement together. Extinction of learning occurs when the reinforcement is discontinued after some time and learning material is presented alone without the corresponding reinforcement. The learner learns to distinguish between material which is accompanied by reinforcement and the material which is not accompanied by reinforcement. Finally, some stimuli which are closely associated with reinforcements may themselves become reinforcing stimuli — e.g., money, grades and other rewards.

The impact of behavioral theory on American education is enormous. The concepts espoused by this theory can be seen in the development of the notion of behavioral objectives and the teaching methods such as programmed learning, Computer-Assisted Instruction (CAI), and Personalized System of Instruction (PSI). The basic notion behind these methods is that learning material can be broken down into simpler units (e.g., frames in programmed instruction) and that mastery of these units leads to mastery of the subject matter. The reinforcement mechanism, typically, in these methods is the opportunity for the learner to advance to the next learning unit and/or earning a grade. In general, many of these techniques allow the learner to proceed at his/her own pace. Similarly, the practice of setting behavioral objectives for the learners reflects the behaviorists' emphasis on observable behaviors. Consequently, behavioral objectives emphasize the notion that learning has occurred only when it is reflected in observable and measurable behaviors.

IB. Cognitive Theory

While behaviorism rejected mentalistic explanations for learning, cognitive theory assumes the presence of a mind which is responsible for learning.[6] While behavioral theory is based on reductionism, cognitive theory is holistic in that it believes that the whole is greater than the sum of its parts. The cognitive theory has its origins in the writings of rationalistic philosophers such as Descartes, Leibnitz, and Kant. It is developed by Gestalt psychologists such as Wertheimer, Wolfgang Kohler, and Kurt Kofka, and field theorists such as Kurt Lewin.

The basic assumption of cognitive theory is the existence of mind with its innate structure and organizational properties. The mind is assumed to play a significant role in learning. The mind is endowed with a structure, called cognitive structure, which is in-born with built-in capacities and limitations; the cognitive structure is primary and precedes experience; and the primary function of mind is abstraction. Some evidence for the mind's innate properties comes from the children's ability in forming complex sentences which they never heard before. Indirect evidence lies in the fact that an organism is bombarded with thousands of stimuli. However, the organism responds to only a part of those stimuli ignoring the others. It is suggested that it is the mind which is responsible for screening out the unwanted stimuli and enabling the organism to concentrate on the others. Similarly, even children display the notion of causality. That is, when two events A and B occur together, they ascribe that event B is caused by event A instead of assuming that these two events are independent of each other. Studies in the area of perception offer some of the strongest evidence for the role of mind in learning. Jean Piaget's concept of schema, Michael Polanyi's concepts of focal and subsidiary awareness and Noam Chomsky's work on linguistics contributed to the understanding of mental structures. The information storage, processing and retrieval capabilities of computers provided significant understanding of human memory and contributed to the acceptance of cognitive perspective.

Cognitive theorists maintain that learning is best facilitated when the learner has an "understanding" of the task to be learned. Understanding is the learner's "awareness of relationships between parts and whole, [and] of means to consequences."[7] Gestalt theorists, for instance, maintain that "insight," where a learner suddenly discovers the solution to a problem, is more a result of understanding rather than simple trial and error discovery, the explanation favored by behaviorists. Understanding of a learning situation helps the learner to transfer the learning to novel situations where the learner can grasp the similarities of relationships. For instance, it is easier to learn a set of syllables if they are grouped according to a discernible pattern than a set of nonsense syllables. Similarly, once the learner understands the pattern, he/she will be able to solve a similar problem even though the relationships may not be exactly the same.

The most important factors which influence learning are: (1) what and how well the learner already knows; and (2) if the learning task is related to the learner's existing knowledge. For learning to take place, the learning material must be "meaningful" to the learner in that the learning material must be related to what the learner already knows.[8] The learner "understands" the learning material if he/she can establish subordinate or superordinate relationships between the learning material and the concepts he/she already knows.[9] A subordinate realtionship exists when the learning material is a specific instance of a concept the learner already knows. A superordinate relationship exists when several concepts which exist in the learner's mind are seen as specific examples of a concept represented

18

by the learning material. Piaget explains this phenomena in terms of assimilation and accommodation.

Learning can be improved by following four specific techniques of presenting the subject matter.[10] First, the learner is presented with the most general and inclusive ideas before being presented with detailed information.[11] These general ideas, called advance organizers, help the learner "categorize, pigeonhole, and inter-relate" the subsequently presented detailed information. Second, the learner's attention is explicitly drawn to the connections be-tween the new learning material and the material the learner already knows. Third, the learning material is presented in a sequential man-ner in which the new material logically depends upon the previously presented material. Fourth, the learner is introduced to the new learning material only after he/she mastered the previous material.

The influence of cognitive perspective on American education can be seen in the reforms that science education has gone through after the Russians launched Sputnik 1 in October 1957. The resul-tant concern on the state of American science education led the federal government to fund curriculum study committees such as the Physical Science Study Committee, Biological Sciences Cur-riculum Study, Chemical Education Materials Study and so on. One of these committees, for instance, proposed to teach high school chemistry around the concept of chemical bonds since "the making and breaking of these ties between atoms" is an activity central to the chemical science.[12] It is pointed out that chemical bonds "is a theme large enough to include a great amount of descriptive chemis-try and at the same time to serve as a guide to the items which can best be included in the course itself . . . . A wide variety of com-pounds and related physical and chemical phenomena can then be discussed with reference to the main features of the bond types in-volved."[13] Similar thinking was behind the other science education projects. In all these approaches, the emphasis was on student learning of a few powerful principles which can explain a large number of phenomena as opposed to presenting a series of seeming-ly unconnected phenomena. Another example of the influence of cognitive perspective is the development of survey courses where these courses try to present a coherent picture of the curriculum. Again, such attempts try to develop a cohesive view of the subject matter enabling the student to quickly grasp the interrelationships between various courses he/she would be taking.

II. Learning Theories and Bibliographic Instruction

IIA. Behavioral Theory

The influence of behaviorism on bibliographic instruction has been enormous. In this section we will discuss three of the major products of the behavioral approach: behavioral objectives, workbooks, and objective tests.

Objectives:

Although many library instruction objectives have been published, the most comprehensive set is the "Model Statement of Objectives" (revised and republished in *Bibliographic Instruction Handbook*).[14] The authors specifically relate the objectives to the behavior approach. "An attempt has been made to write the enabling objectives as *behavioral* objectives . . . the objectives should be specific and measurable" (p36). Two examples of these enabling objectives are:

> The student will correcting identify and explain the purpose of selected elements on a sample catalog entry in a specified period of time. The selected elements will include the author, title, place of publication, publisher, date of publication, series title, bibliographic notes, tracings, and call number. (p39)

> In a specified time period, the student can identify major reference tools (encyclopedia, dictionary, index) in a specified field using a guide to the literature such as Sheehy's *Guide to Reference Books*. (p40)

These objectives clearly reflect one of the major tenets of behaviorism that all knowledge can be broken down into basic units. In fact, the whole statement is set up with a general objective, terminal objectives, and enabling objectives such as the two which we quoted. The enabling objectives clearly relate to the idea that learning takes place when observable behavioral change takes place.

Some of the enabling objectives used in this statement are overarching. For instance:

> The student will identify the major channels of scholarly communication within her/his own field of interest and the formats in which this communication appears in the literature.

Unfortunately this type of objective is much less amenable to exact measurement so it is less emphasized than other more measurable objectives.

It is interesting to note that the authors of the model objectives explicitly state that "the primary role of bibliographic instruction is to provide students with the specific skills needed to successfully complete their assignments" (p36). In other words, there is a greater emphasis on "skills" as opposed to concepts.

Workbooks:

Implementation of some of these objectives often has been accomplished by using library skills workbooks based on the model workbook developed by Mimi Dudley at UCLA. These workbooks reflect significantly the fundamental ideas of the behavioral approach. They are set up to help students identify and find specific reference sources and to provide students with the skills needed to use these sources.

In the introduction to Mimi Dudley's 1973 edition of *Workbook in Library Skills* she states: "The assignments are to be completed within a given period of time, and you may proceed at your own pace." The self-paced nature of these workbooks is closely tied to behaviorism. Also, the grading of the workbook is based on completing each answer correctly even if the student has to re-do a question numerous times.

The questions which appear in the workbooks are very specific in nature which is indicative of the behavioral approach. An example from Dudley's workbook shows its specific nature. In the section on biographies this question appears:

> Your somewhat elderly professor of Modern British History has the highly original theory that people who are born in odd-numbered years contribute more to the world than people born in even-numbered years. To verify his theory he has asked each of you to report on a famous person. Using one of the national biographical dictionaries listed in your workbook, you find out when *Sir Winston Churchill* was born. (p38)

Although the question is made interesting by means of a story, its basic purpose still is to locate specific biographical information.

Tests:

Most of the literature on library skills tests deals with tests based on behavioral concepts. Objective tests, often given as pre- and post-tests, abound. These tests are referred to as the "agricultural-botany paradigm" where two groups of students — like plants — are given pre-tests. One group is then given library instruction — or water and food — and then the growth measured.[15]

One example of these tests is found in Wiggins and Low's article in the July, 1972 *Drexel Library Quarterly*. The section of their bibliographic instruction program discussed in the article deals with periodical indexes.[16] They had four terminal objectives, one of which was article selection, and one of the enabling objectives for this terminal objective is to "Identify all parts of an index entry" (p271–272). The test question to measure this knowledge was:

> Find the numbered item in the examples below which fit the description in (a) through (i) and write the number in the blank by the appropriate letter on your answer sheet.

BICYCLES[1]

Look what's happening to bicycles[2]

A. Wall.[3] il.[4] Pop Sci[5] 187:[6] 108--111[7-8] Ag[9] '65[10]

__(a) year   __(f) month
__(b) title of article   __(g) continued page(s)
__(c) title of periodical   __(h) volume number
__(d) author   __(i) page number(s)
__(e) subject

Another example is the test developed at the University of Arizona and reported on by Shelley Phipps and Ruth Dickstein.[17] An example of one of their questions is:

> Question 8: In the Library of Congress Classification system, the letters "HA" in the call number HA67V42 refer to which of the following?
> __ the author's initials
> __ the general subject of the book
> __ the branch library where the book is located
> __ don't know

In these examples of objective tests, many tenets of behaviorism can be seen. Items are broken down into smaller units, and it is assumed that mastery of the smaller units leads to mastery of the subject matter. Behaviorism assumes that learning has taken place when overt, observable change has taken place. If a student is given a pre-test and does not answer a question correctly, but does answer that same question correctly in a post-test, then overt, observable and quantifiable change has taken place.

IIB. Cognitive Theory

Content:

In this section we will discuss what cognitive theory means for the content of bibliographic instruction and what it means for evaluation. According to cognitive learning theory, material should be presented using "unifying concepts and propositions . . . that have the widest explanatory power, inclusiveness, generalizability and reliability . . . ." In librarianship and bibliographic instruction we have a number of unifying concepts which have wide explanatory power. These concepts or conceptual frameworks include systematic literature searching (made famous by Tom Kirk and others), publication sequence, citation patterns, and primary and secondary sources.

To elaborate on this idea of unifying concepts or advance organizers, I will use the framework of primary and secondary sources. The explanation of primary sources as those which report on original research is fundamental for a discussion of the excitement of original work, the research process, various types of creative work, etc. Advanced students who need to use primary sources for their own work would be particularly attuned to this information. Secondary sources can be introduced as those which provide access to and explain primary sources.

As an example, in the field of urban studies primary sources include journal articles and conference papers as is typical in all social scientific research. Primary sources also include what Freides and Werking[19] would refer to as data sources, such material as census and other demographic information, and statistical sources on employment, income, etc. A broad spectrum and many examples of important types of material fall into the category of primary sources for urban studies.

Secondary sources, which rearrange or explain primary material, relate to the already introduced primary sources in urban studies. *American Statistical Index* is a secondary source which provides access to census and statistical sources, as is the *Statistical Reference Index*. Journal articles can be identified by using *Urban Affairs Abstracts* and other indexes, and conference papers are identified by *Index to Proceedings in the Social Sciences and Humanities*. Books and encyclopedias are other examples of secondary sources.

This kind of conceptual framework or advance organizer also

helps to establish the subordinate and superordinate relationships which cognitive theorists state are important for learning. After the learner is introduced to journal articles as primary sources, he or she can subsume a specific journal, for instance, *Architectural Digest*, as one example of that category. On the other hand, advanced urban studies students might well know of *Public Affairs Information Service* and be better prepared to understand the major purposes of abstract journals and periodical indexes, thus establishing a superordinate relationship.

Let us leave the example of primary/secondary sources as an advance organizer, and proceed to some other examples of what cognitive learning theory means for the content of bibliographic instruction.

Cognitive learning theory states that to make material meaningful it should be related to what the learner already knows. Or, as Morton Hunt in a *New York Times Magazine* article says, "in everyday life we reason most of the time by noting similarities between things, making good guesses and reaching conclusions on the basis of likelihood or probability."[20] Libraries and their materials and organization are very well suited to explanation by relating ideas to what students already know. For instance, I have found that in Freshmen English composition classes, students will invariably be able to tell me that magazine articles are necessary because they are current. Students can easily absorb the idea that current research and scholarly articles can be found in journals, just as current news, political, and social information can be found in magazine and newspaper articles.

I also have found that most freshmen have heard or or used *Readers' Guide to Periodical Literature*. That means it is easier for them, by establishing a superordinate relationship, to understand the purpose and nature of periodical indexes. One other example on this idea of relating meaning to existing knowledge: I was teaching a freshmen class one day and realized that the students were less than enthralled as I talked about the elements of an entry in a periodical index. Suddenly inspiration hit, and I told the students this was the exact information they needed for their bibliographies. The class really became alert and asked many questions because of relating information to something they had heard about and needed to know more about.

Evaluation:

In cognitive theory, evaluation should measure whether students have understood concepts and principles and relationships between concepts. Some possible evaluative instruments include bibliographies and pathfinders, especially with essays explaining why certain sources were chosen. Essay examinations are another possibility. The essay questions need to be based on comparisons, purposes, and generalizations. Even some carefully designed objective tests may be structured to test for concepts. It is interesting to note in this connection the criticism voiced by the students of Georgia Institute of Technology on objective tests. They correlated the increasing use of objective tests with the decline in the quality of instruction at Georgia Institute of Technology. The students preferred essay type of examinations to objective tests.

Conclusion

The purpose of our paper has been to explain behaviorism and cognitive theory and their impact — past and potential — on bibliographic instruction. We have tried to bridge the gap between theory and practice, and we have separated ideas from their influences in order to emphasize both. However, both behavioral and cognitive learning theories have much to offer to bibliographic education. Our students need both skills, which seem to be emphasized in the behavioral model, and concepts, which seem to be predominant in cognitive theory. For librarians, formulation of objectives is beneficial for clarifying what we hope to accomplish while looking at overall concepts helps to identify what really is important to teach and to learn. Cognitive theory is experiencing a wide popularity now, much as behaviorism did until recently. It will be interesting to see what continued effects cognitive theory may have on bibliographic instruction. If our bibliographic education curriculum places more emphasis on broad principles, then we will nicely complement reference desk service. The reference desk is the better place to reinforce specifics, while the bibliographic instruction class is the better place to set the framework for library research.

Further, cognitive theory with its emphasis on concepts may help librarians to get closer to some of the fundamental premises inherent in our field. It is beneficial to look at the whole instead of the parts as we so often do. Getting down — or up to the essential principles is particularly necessary because of the impact of computers on libraries and librarianship. We look forward to continuing research in this area; it will be interesting to see what the future holds.

Acknowledgments

The authors gratefully acknowledge the assistance of Dr. Alan Goldman whose critical comments on the manuscript were invaluable.

Notes

1. The section on learning theories is largely based on Bower, Gordon H. and Ernest R. Hilgrad, *Theories of Learning*, 5th ed. (Englewood Cliffs, NJ: Prentice-Hall, 1981).

2. Wingfield, Arthur. *Human Learning and Memory: An Introduction* (New York: Harper & Row, 1979) p3.

3. Bower and Hilgrad, op.cit., p2–3.

4. Wingfield, op.cit., p122.

5. Ibid., p119–122.

6. Bower and Hilgrad, op.cit., p4–8.

7. Ibid., p322.

8. Ausubel, David P. *Educational Psychology: A Cognitive View* (New York: Holt, Rinehart & Winston, 1968) p37--38.

9. Ibid., p152–160.

10. Ibid., p152–160.

11. Bower and Hilgrad, op.cit., p540.

12. Strong, Lawrence E. and M. Kent Wilson. "Chemical Bonds: A Central Theme for High School Chemistry." *Journal of Chemical Education* 35 (1958): 56–58.

13. Ibid., p56.

14. "Academic Bibliographic Instruction: Model Statement of Objectives" in *Bibliographic Instruction Handbook* (Chicago: American Library Association, 1980) p35--45.

15. Werking, Richard Hume. "Evaluating Bibliographic Education: A Review and Critique." *Library Trends* 29 (Summer 1980): 153–172.

16. Wiggins, Marvin E. and D. Stewart Low. "Use of an Instructional Psychology Model for Development of Library-Use Instructional Programs." *Drexel Library Quarterly* 8 (July 1972): 269--279.

17. Phipps, Shelley and Ruth Dickstein. "The Library Skills Program at the University of Arizona: Testing, Evaluation, and Critique." *Journal of Academic Librarianship* 5 (September 1979): 205--214.

18. Ausubel, op.cit., p147.

19. Freides, Thelma. *Literature and Bibliography of the Social Sciences* (Los Angeles: Melville, 1973) and Werking, Richard, "Course Related Instruction for History Majors" in Kirkendall, Carolyn A., ed. *Putting Library Instruction in Its Place: In the Library and in the Library School.* Library Orientation Series, no. 8 (Ann Arbor, MI: Pierian Press, 1978) p44--47.

20. Hunt, Morton. "How the Mind Works." *New York Times Magazine* (January 24, 1982): 30–33+.

LEARNING LIBRARY SKILLS IN AUSTRALIA
– WHERE TO NOW?

Megan Lilly
Chisholm Institute

My premise will be that user education in Australia underwent a period of expansion and development in the 1960s and early 1970s. That development was paralleled and partly caused by an expansion in the tertiary education system.

Since the early 1970s, user education has consolidated its position in our education system. However, I believe that very soon user education will be on the defensive because of the severe cuts in funding in the tertiary education sector in Australia.

I will start with some background on the Australian education system with which you may not be familiar. Australia has 19 universities and had approximately 90 colleges of advanced education – now closer to 50, due to amalgamations. The universities run degree programmes up to and including doctorate level and are heavily involved in research. The colleges of advanced education conduct three and four year degree and diploma courses, and some offer masters degrees. The colleges evolved from institutes of technology and from teacher training colleges: their role is, therefore, as providers of education in the applied arts and sciences with little emphasis on research.

All these institutions in the tertiary sector, perhaps with the exception of church-run religious training colleges, are funded by the federal government. Some of the universities do have income from investments and endowments, but this source of income is a very small part of their overall budgets. Tuition fees are not charged in Australia for undergraduate degrees if it is the first degree or for post-graduate qualifications which are vocational, such as the one-year full-time post-graduate diploma which is the usual library qualification and the equivalent of the American MLS.

University education in Australia expanded in the late 1950s and 1960s as a result of an expanding economy and the demand for education created by the post-war baby boom. The colleges of advanced education had their turn in the late 1960s and early 1970s and it is from these colleges that the major advances in user education in Australia came, for a number of reasons.

Firstly, the colleges of advanced education were new. Rapid expansion meant large increases in staffing. Young librarians were given an opportunity to rise more quickly in the ranks and they came from library schools with new ideas which were allowed scope in the expanding system. The openings available for librarians in this system is illustrated by the fact that of the seven largest colleges in Melbourne, five have chief librarians who are forty-five years old or younger, though none of them is female, which is another story.

The colleges, then, led the way in user education in Australia in the early years. However, there is now no significant difference between the two parts of the tertiary education sector, and I will treat them as one for the purposes of this discussion.

My next question is — What has happened to user education since its rise in Australia in the late 1960s and early 1970s?

Andrew White from the Western Australia Institute of Technology conducted a survey of 52 universities and colleges in 1973.[1] In 1981, Patrick Condon, the Institute Librarian at my college, and I conducted a small survey of randomly selected colleges and universities. To facilitate comparison we asked the same questions that Andrew White asked.

The results of these surveys indicate that the last eight years have been a period of consolidation in user education in Australia. We seem to have a solid acceptance of user education in tertiary institutions, though the emphasis is still on undergraduate programs.

The Question Is — Where to Now?

Along with other western governments, Australia's federal government is cutting public expenditure in an attempt to control inflation. Education, along with other social services, is being funded less now than it was five years ago, or even two years ago. For Australia's tertiary education sector, the honeymoon is over. Most universities and colleges are struggling to hold ground: expansion is no longer an issue — survival is.

The Australian Government's Review of Administrative Services (known locally as the "Razor Gang") has recommended widespread cuts in education funding as well as pressuring institutions in the tertiary sector to cut student numbers and to amalgamate with other institutions. In my state of Victoria alone, eight colleges of advanced education have been forced to amalgamate to form three new colleges, and one large teacher training college has been threatened with closure if it does not find an amalgamation partner by the end of this year.

These changes happened very quickly — they were announced in May 1981 and all the amalgamations were in effect by March this year, except the one mentioned above.

The effect has been traumatic, to put it mildly. Libraries in the amalgamating colleges are being forced to rationalise staffing levels, and redundancy among librarians is likely to become a fact of life.

Coupled with these amalgamations are the cuts in funding which are affecting all tertiary institutions. At Chisholm Institute, for instance, there has been an overall six percent cut in funds this year, which seems to be an average figure across the college sector.

In the past, these types of cuts tend to be made in the goods and services section of an institute's budget. But there is now pressure on administrations to make cuts in staffing or recurrent costs, which at Chisholm make up about 87 percent of the total institute budget. Due to pressure from the academic staff, these cuts are likely to be made in the non-academic staff areas. Patrick Condon, Institute Librarian at Chisholm, believes that some college libraries will be facing a real cut of 15 percent in their budgets.

The amalgamations and the funding cuts will force many academic libraries to take a close look at their services and their staff, and unless we are vigilant, user education may become a casualty.

There are a number of reasons why I believe this may be the case.

Firstly, within the library there will be less staff, and each staff member will be expected to do more. This seems to be a traditional response in service areas: everyone is loath to cut services to users. However, in Australia, user education is a labour intensive activity. For instance, during 1981, at Chisholm Institute we conducted 230 hours of user education and covered a little under 3,000 students. That figure does not include preparation time, which would increase it by at least half. Most of those 230 hours were actual classroom contact hours as opposed to practical sessions, and represent one person's full-time work for over six weeks, again excluding preparation time.

I believe that we must reduce the man-hours involved in conducting user education, but how? Technology springs to mind, but again we in Australia are going to have problems. Few academic libraries in Australian colleges have automated circulation systems, let alone automated user education packages: if there is money available for capital equipment, it will be spent in technical services rather than user services areas.

Part of the solution lies in making use of techniques of learning which do not involve librarians in a teaching role quite as much but which are effective for the learner.

Vivien Nash from Monash University, Melbourne, has produced

a library skills workbook for geography students (one copy in LOEX), which may be one type of solution.

At Chisholm Institute, we decided to combine our informal user education (or orientation) with basic formal user education by giving students an exercise to complete in their first one-hour session, rather than offering tours in Orientation Week and a lecture on the catalogues and other information retrieval tools in the first week of semester as we have done in the past.

The overall aim of the exercise was to introduce students to basic information retrieval skills while familiarising them with the layout of the library.

Each part of the exercise was designed to cover an element of information retrieval or orientation which has seemed in the past to be a stumbling block to new students.

These elements are:

a) distinguishing between the functions of the author-title and subject catalogues;
b) writing down the call number in full;
c) finding the material on Level 4, i.e., realising that there is a Level 4;
d) filling in a loan card;
e) finding a periodical using the periodical strip index;
f) using the reference collection as a separate collection;
g) distinguishing between the services offered at the "ASK ME" desk, the Enquiries desk and the Loan Enquiries counter;
h) using the Reserve collection;
i) knowing where to look for library opening hours.

Objectives

The exercise was designed to fulfill the following objectives:

After library orientation, the student should be able to:

1. locate a book using the author and title catalogue;

2. fill out a loan card correctly, including imprinting their name and number on the loan card;

3. locate a book using the subject catalogue;

4. locate an English dictionary in the reference collection when given the call number;

32

5. locate a periodical using the periodical strip index;

6. locate an audio visual item using the author and title catalogue and be able to collect the relevant equipment from the Enquiries desk; and

7. identify some of the services offered by the Library at the "ASK ME" desk, the Loan Enquiries counter, the Reserve counter and Inter-Library loans.

Preparation

Preparation for the "Take a Tour" exercise was fairly time consuming. However, the time involved in making the signs for the exercise is a "once only" cost as they are re-usable.

The exercise was designed with blank elements in the questions which had to be filled in before the exercise was distributed. This was both tedious and time consuming, but was necessary to ensure that each student doing the exercise would be looking for different materials.

The questions on the exercise sheet were also in a different order (four different combinations in some cases) to help prevent bottlenecks at service points.

Target

The exercise was run as a pilot with students from Marketing, Finance and Law, and Humanities. Eighty-five students did the exercise, and as a result the exercise was shortened and some of the questions were reworded slightly.

The revised "Take a Tour" exercise was used with 202 Business students, 29 Humanities students and 104 Art and Design students. The Art and Design version was shortened and simplified yet again, which is reflected in those students' responses to the question "Do you think the questions in the "Take a Tour" exercise were easy, just right or difficult?"

Evaluation

No attempt was made to quantify the students' performance on the exercise. However, each exercise was perused by the librarian responsible before being returned to the students.

The responses of students to the exercise are tabulated in percentages in Appendix 1.

Overall, the response was good, and was remarkably consistent over the three groups of students, except for question 3. As I mentioned above, the Art & Design students had a modified (easier?) version of the exercise, and this is reflected in their response to question 3. Leaving out the Art & Design responses, the mean responses to this question are:

Easy	17%
Just Right	75.5%
Difficult	7%

which indicates that the level of difficulty of the exercise as perceived by the students was appropriate.

The responses to question 5 were consistent across the three groups and heartening: at least *they* thought they had learned something! And, 82 percent enjoyed doing it (see question 1).

Educationally speaking our main problem with the exercise was quantifying the students' performances, or not quantifying them, as was the case. The design of the exercise, with some open ended questions, made marking in a formal sense impossible, although our overall impression was that most students handled the exercise quite well.

With reference to Ellison's factors which significantly influence learning,[2] we found:

1. the students were motivated to do the exercise for two reasons: the lecturer in charge of the subject had stressed to them the importance of knowing how to use the library *for that subject*, and the tasks in the exercise were related to the students' immediate needs (albeit as perceived by the lecturer);

2. students were able to relate the tasks they were asked to perform to their needs (making "meaningful relationships") because the questions were posed in terms of the problem — for example, the question involving use of the subject catalogue was headed "Finding a book when you do not know the author or the title." At each stage in the exercise we tried to ensure that the students knew *why* they were doing a particular task;

3. style helps a lot! In keeping with our policy of friendly service we tried to inject an air of informality (not frivolity) into the exercise. A librarian met the students and briefly explained the exercise before they started, and it was impressed upon them they could ask for help at any stage. All the signs

connected with the exercise were colour coded in bold green and were decorated with green footprints to tie them in with the "Take a Tour" brochure which accompanied the exercise (in fact the exercist became known as the "green feet exercise"!).

As part of the exercise students were asked to photocopy the title page of a relevant journal (which was specified). When they handed in the completed exercise they received a 5 cent refund (which raised a few eyebrows) and a copy of the library guide. They were then asked to complete the evaluation questionnaire (anonymously), which was explained as their chance to get revenge! Most students took it in good part, as the results of the questionnaire show.

Needless to say there were problems. Preparation of the exercise sheets was more time consuming than we anticipated. Future pressures on staff as a result of the developments I outlined earlier in this paper will not give us the same opportunity to vary the content of the questions as we did this first time, and the students performance in the exercise must be quantified if we are to be able to justify even this level of user education activity.

In conclusion I would reiterate that it is in the direction of guided self-learning that user education in Australia must head. We hope we've made an appropriate start with our "Take a Tour" exercise.

Notes

1. White, Andrew. *Survey of Reader Education in Tertiary Institutions in Australia, 1973.* Sydney: Universities & Colleges Section, LAA, 1974.

2. Ellison, John W. "Effective Library Instruction and the Learning Process." *Catholic Library World* 53 (4), November, 1981.

APPENDIX 1

Questionnaire
(results in percentages)

1. Did you enjoy answering the questions in the "Take a Tour" exercise?

	Bus.	Hums.	A&D	Mean
Yes	77	86	82	82
No	22	14	16	17
Undecided	1	—	2	1

2. Do you think the "Take a Tour" exercise is a good method of learning about use of the library?

	Bus.	Hums.	A&D	Mean
Not good	2	0	1	1
Satisfactory	16	14	17	16
Good	40	38	33	37
Very good	41	48	49	46
Excellent	.5			—

3. Do you think the questions in the "Take a Tour" exercise were:

	Bus.	Hums.	A&D	Mean
Easy	20	14	40	25
Just right	75	76	55	69
Difficult	4	10	6	7
Undecided	1			—

4. Do you think the amount of time involved in completing the "Take a Tour" exercise was —

	Bus.	Hums.	A&D	Mean
Too short	5	10	10	8
Just right	70	83	78	77
Too long	23	7	11	14
Undecided	2			—

5. Do you think you learned anything useful about the library by doing this exercise?

	Bus.	Hums.	A&D	Mean
Yes	94	100	90	95
No	6	—	9	5
Undecided			1	

6. Do you have any comments, criticisms or suggestions to make about the "Take a Tour" exercise?

Please write them here:

MOTIVATION
AND THE LIBRARY LEARNER

Morell D. Boone
Eastern Michigan University

The purpose of this presentation is to describe a theoretical approach to understanding motivation in relation to other factors that influence learning and the design of instruction.

The paper begins from an historical perspective with the major influences in instructional design that have come before the consideration of motivation. The second portion introduces an instructional analysis model for the purpose of developing an applied context for considering motivational factors in a learning situation. The last portion introduces an example of a theoretical development process that culminates in an operational information search model constructed as a basis for incorporating and expanding two motivational theories. It is not meant to be an exhaustive treatment, but an introduction to the consideration of an individual's motivation in a learning situation.

Up to now, we have not given adequate systematic attention to the problem of an individual's motivation, either in bibliographic instruction or instruction in general. Motivation is generally defined as that which accounts for the arousal, direction and continuance of behavior.

Since bibliographic instruction is in the early stages of having a theory of instructional design all its own, we need to address the question of learner's motivation within a parallel context. The one chosen for this presentation is that of instructional design within the field of instructional technology.

Historical Perspective

Historically, instructional design efforts had a strong emphasis on the applications of behavioral psychology. This approach resulted in the use of many types of contingency management systems, including programmed instruction, contingency contracting and personalized instructional systems.[1] Many of these instructional systems were based on the assumption that behavior is controlled by its consequences   and that heavy reinforcement of positive responses is necessary.

While behavioral theory explains some of what happens in learning, these assumptions were found by many not to be sufficient. The abilities and the characteristics of human information processing were added to the behavioral assumptions. Consequently, assumptions of cognitive psychology, including information processing theory, individual different theory, and communications theory, were included.[2] A relatively new focus on stimulus characteristics usually incorporates the interaction of individual abilities and skills. For example, one such major approach that has been developed is known as aptitude-treatment-interaction research.[3]

Relatively speaking, we can say that instructional design now incorporates tenets and practices derived from behavioral psychology and cognitive learning psychology. Where great progress has been made in incorporating these two basic psychologies, it is less evident that the motives of the learner have been taken into account in instructional design efforts.

The motives of an individual (i.e., motivational factors), can be divided into two categories of behavior. The first is Performance; it refers to the actual accomplishment of a required task. The second is Effort; it refers to whether the individual engaged in action is trying to accomplish the task. Where performance is measured by referencing it to a standard with respect to a goal, effort is measured in terms of persistence. Since effort is measured by persistence, it is a direct indicator of motivation. It is this definition of motivation that is of primary value to the theoretical approach addressed in this presentation. One of the best sources for information about concepts of, and measures of motivation is an ERIC publication by Keller, Kelly and Dodge.[4]

Instructional Analysis Model

Before we look at a theoretical basis for explaining an individual's motivation in a learning situation, it is desirable to know what would be the relevance to bibliographic instruction practitioners in knowing more about this subject. To do this, it might be helpful to view a model of instructional analysis described in Figure 1.[5] The first step in the model is to identify and to be able to analyze the underlying motivational problem in terms of type and location. It must be stressed that this is only one type of instructional problem. Others (e.g., abilities, skills and styles) could be substituted for motivation in such a model.

There are three general types of motivational problems in two

38

locations as defined in this model. The first of the two types of motivational problems consists of the extent to which the learner perceives the instruction to be relevant and interesting (value terms) and possible (expectancy terms). The third type concerns how to avoid negative cognitive evaluation regarding the outcomes of the instruction. That is, in order to motivate learners, their curiosity must be aroused in combination with their perception of relevancy to their personal goals, and they must perceive that the success in learning is possible within the context of outcomes of the learning experience being consistent with their own reasons for learning.

The location of the problem may be in the learner or in the instruction, or a combination of the two. If the problem is within the learner, we say that the individual might be low in relevant motive, or might be low in personal expectancy for success.

In contrast, the problem might lie in the instruction. Of course, this never happens within bibliographic instruction. No one has ever developed a technique for being boring, have they? However, it is probably safe to say that we do not always pay strict attention to the relevancy, level of difficulty and desired outcomes in the material we present. However, it is really too simplistic to say that the problem lies in just one source or the other. Usually, the problem's causality can be identified to some degree in both sources, especially when it comes to subject matter that is not commonly thought of as being x-rated.

The second step in the process is to design appropriate motivational strategies in relation to the three problem areas. For example, a learning situation should contain conditions that encourage curiosity and address the issue of providing information that is relevant from the learner's perspective. Another example of motivational design concerns the perception of desired outcomes from the instructor's and learner's point of view. That is, if there is a difference of opinion in evaluating success, there would be a potential problem in the learner's continuing motivation regarding the learning situation.

To complete the model, steps 3 and 4 are necessary. These are provisions for implementation and evaluation of the approach.

Now that we have looked at the historical developments and the applied context, it is time to examine a theoretical basis for considering the motivational factors identified under the types of problems in the instructional analysis model. For this we turn to my own research[6] which is described in the abstract contained in Appendix A.

Theoretical Model Development

An information search model (figure 2), derived from the two theoretical approaches and set in an expectancy-value framework,

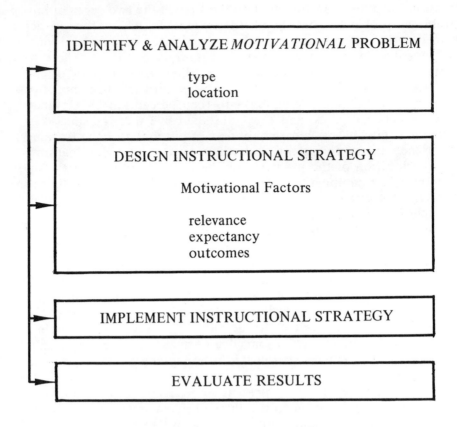

Figure 1. Instructional Analysis Model

was tested in a study that involved a voluntary group of 32 students enrolled in a library skills course who were asked to select a topic for a bibliographic assignment. Information search is defined here as the activity of seeking, acquiring and processing information from the environment before a decision is made.[7]

Rotter's social learning theory was selected as the theoretical framework.[8] It was selected for the following reasons:

a) It contains a detailed explanation of concepts that account for the prediction of human behavior;
b) it uses a limited number of explanatory concepts;
c) it has a sizeable amount of empirical support, especially in the development of a measurement concept, an instrument for the expectancy component;
d) it is generalizable to the study of information-search behavior

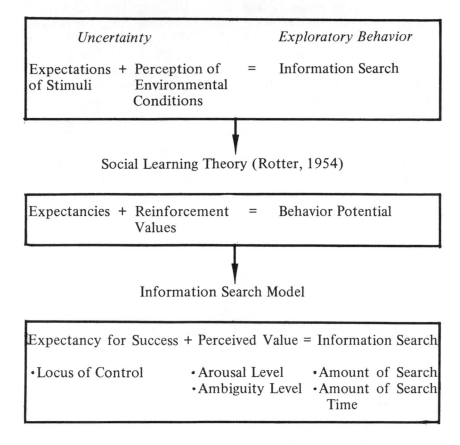

Conflict-Arousal Theory (Berlyne, 1960)

Uncertainty		*Exploratory Behavior*
Expectations + Perception of = Information Search		
of Stimuli Environmental		
Conditions		

Social Learning Theory (Rotter, 1954)

Expectancies + Reinforcement = Behavior Potential
Values

Information Search Model

Expectancy for Success + Perceived Value = Information Search

•Locus of Control   •Arousal Level   •Amount of Search
                        •Ambiguity Level •Amount of Search
                                           Time

Figure 2. Derivation of the Information Search Model

    which considers valuables from both drive and cognitive theories;

e) it is a current theory with clearly-stated principles and descriptions, which have been used by many researchers for a wide variety of person and environment interaction studies.

    Berlyne's conflict arousal theory is used as a further delineation of Rotter's concept of perceived value.[9] According to Berlyne, a drive state of conflict is created by a condition of uncertainty which is influenced by both extrinsic (i.e., environment) and instinsic (i.e., person) factors.

    The three categories of motivational constructs (figure 3) derived from social learning theory are identical to the constructs identified in the instructional analysis model discussed earlier. The first component is behavior potential and this is synonymous with outcomes. For the purpose of the work being described here, the amount of information search and search time which is a result of effort to reach a decision or goal put forth by an individual is the desired outcome. The other two constructs are expectancies and values or relevance. Expectancies are the subject of probabilities of successful choices in information search. Values, on the other hand, are an individual's perception of the level of arousal caused by uncertainty and the importance or strength of competing responses of information in a choice situation. The behavior potential outcome was identified as information search which was represented by the amount of search and the amount of search time. The first independent variable, expectancy for success, was represented as an individual's locus of control (i.e., internal or external orientation). The second independent variable, perceived value, was represented by an individual's preferred arousal level (i.e., high or low) and his or her preferred ambiguity level (i.e., tolerance or intolerance).

The model was then operationalized and tested (figure 4). Specifically, the model was used to answer the question: Is motivation, operationally defined as effort expended and time spent in information search, related to an individual's expectancy for success and perceived value of goal?

The decision task (i.e., topic selection) required effort or persistence in order to reach an outcome (i.e., information search

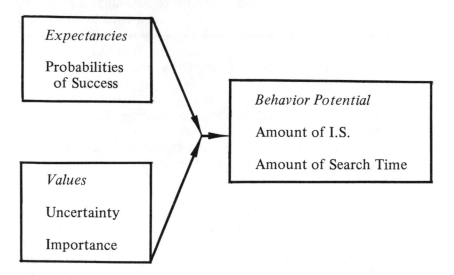

Figure 3. Motivational Constructs

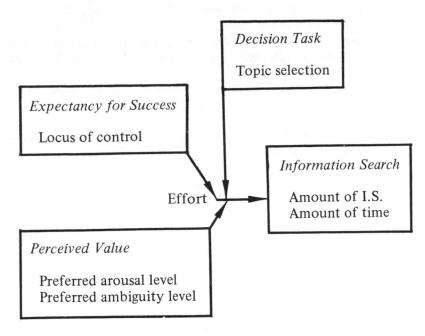

Figure 4. Operational Model

measured by number of sources used and number of weeks to complete task) and both expectancies for success (i.e., measured by locus of control score) and perceived value (i.e., measured by preferred arousal level score minus preferred ambiguity level score) were predictors of the amount of effort or motivation exerted in information search.

This unique and limited study, based on an expectancy-value information search model, has been presented for your consideration in the hope that it will motivate, or at least interest you in exploring further this important component of a learner's behavior. It is one example of the usefulness of motivational constructs in predicting the amount of effort a learner expends when faced with a decision task.

In conclusion, your willingness to consider the importance of motivational constructs (i.e., expectancies, values and outcomes) of the library learner in a learning situation is respectfully requested. The reading list contained in Appendix B was prepared for further exploration into the theories presented here, and also to provide an opportunity for a broader-based investigation of person-environment motivational concerns, both from learner and instructional perspectives.

Notes

1. Snelbecker, G.E. *Learning Theory, Instructional Theory, and Psychoeducational Design*. New York: McGraw-Hill, 1974.

2. Gagne, R.M. *The Conditions of Learning*. 3rd ed. New York: Holt, Rinehart and Winston, 1977.

3. Cronbach, L.J. and R.E. Snow. *Aptitudes and Instructional Methods*. New York: Irvington, 1976.

4. Keller, J.M., E.F. Kelly, and B. Dodge. *A Practitioner's Guide to Concepts and Measures of Motivation*. Syracuse University: ERIC Clearinghouse for Information Resources, 1978.

5. Keller, J.M. "Motivation and Instructional Design: A Theoretical Perspective." *Journal of Instructional Development* no. 4, 2 (Summer 1979).

6. Boone, M.D. "Expectancies and Values as Predictors of Motivation of Pre-Decisional Information Search." Doctoral Dissertation, Syracuse University, 1980. *Dissertation Abstracts International* no. 2 42 (1981). University Microfilms No. 81-14156.

7. Bruner, J.S., J. Goodnow, and G.A. Austin. *A Study of Thinking*. New York: Wiley, 1956.

8. Rotter, J.B., J.E. Chance, and E.J. Phares, eds. *Application of Social Learning Theory of Personality*. New York: Holt, Rinehart and Winston, 1972.

9. Berlyne, D.E. *Conflict, Arousal, and Curiosity*. New York: McGraw-Hill, 1960.

EXPECTANCIES AND VALUES AS PREDICTORS
OF MOTIVATION OF PRE-DECISIONAL
INFORMATION SEARCH

Morell Douglas Boone, Ph.D.
Syracuse University, 1980. 167p.

The principal objective of this investigation was to systematically explore the possible functional relationship between two variables, expectancy for success and perceived value and their predicted effort upon two dependent variables, amount of effort in information search and time spent by individuals in information search. This particular field study is significant in that it describes the relationships between these motivational variables and pre-decisional search behaviors in an actual task situation. Further, it serves to examine Berlyne's (1960) conflict-arousal theory and Rotter's (1954) social learning theory as they apply to predicting motivation of information search. Finally, it provides a conceptual paradigm for educators to investigate a learner's amount of effort expended in information search activity. Specifically, the study attempts to answer the following question: is motivation, operationally defined as effort expended and time spent in information search, related to an individual's expectancy for success and perceived value of goal? To answer this question, a specific expectancy-value model was formulated to test two hypotheses which predicted that an individual's greater or lesser amount of effort in search and time spent in search was a function of the two independent variables.

A voluntary group of 32 students enrolled in a library skills course were asked to select a topic for a tentative bibliography assignment. The two dependent variables were measured by an Information Search Record procedure. Expectancy for success was measured as an individual's locus of control score. Perceived value of goal was measured as an individual's preferred arousal level score minus his/her preferred ambiguity level score. A test was used to analyze the observed mean differences in the scores for the amount of effort in search. These mean differences were found to be statistically significant and were in support of the research hypotheses. Specifically, it was found that individuals who tended to be internally oriented and high in their perceived value, and individuals who tended to be externally oriented and low in their perceived value both expended greater effort in information search activity. Conversely, for individuals who tended to be internally oriented and low in their perceived value and individuals who tended to be externally oriented and high in their perceived value, both experienced lesser effort in search. A chi-square analysis was used to test the statistical significance of mean differences with dichotomous groups of scores for the amount of time spent in search.

These mean differences were found to be statistically significant and were in support of the research hypotheses. Specifically, it was found that for those individuals who tended to be externally oriented and low in their perceived value, and for those individuals who tended to be internally oriented and low in their perceived value, both spent the greatest amount of time in information search activity. Conversely, for those individuals shown to be externally oriented and high in their perceived value, and who were shown to be internally oriented and high in their perceived value, both spent the least amount of time in searching for information.

Appendix B

MOTIVATION – BASIC BOOKS

Atkinson, J.W. *An Introduction to Motivation.* Princeton: Van Nostrand, 1964.

Berlyne, D.E. *Conflict, Arousal, and Curiosity.* New York: McGraw-Hill, 1960.

Berlyne, D.E. *Structure and Direction in Thinking.* New York: Wiley, 1965.

Boone, M.D. "Expectancies and Values as Predictors of Motivation of Predecisional Information Search." Doctoral Dissertation, Syracuse University, 1980. *Dissertation Abstracts International,* no. 2 42 (1981), University Microfilms No. 81--14156.

Bruner, J.S., J. Goodnow, and G.A. Austin. *A Study of Thinking.* New York: Wiley, 1956.

Day, H.I., D.E. Berlyne and D.E. Hunt, eds. *Intrinsic Motivation: A New Direction in Education.* Toronto: Holt, Rinehart and Winston of Canada, 1971.

Feather, N.T. *Values in Education and Society.* New York: The Free Press, 1975.

Hunt, D.E. & Sullivan, E.V. *Between Psychology and Education.* Hinsdale, IL: Dryden Press, 1974.

Joyce, B. and M. Weil. *Models of Teaching.* Englewood Cliffs, NJ: Prentice-Hall, 1972.

Keller, J.M., E.F. Kelly and B. Dodge. *A Practitioner's Guide to Concepts and Measures of Motivation.* Syracuse, NY: Syracuse University, ERIC Clearinghouse for Information Resources, 1978.

Lefcourt, H.M. *Locus of Control.* New York: Wiley, 1976.

Mehrabian, A. and J.A. Russell. *An Approach to Environmental Psychology.* Cambridge, MA: MIT Press, 1974.

Mischel, W. *Introduction to Personality.* 2d ed. New York: Holt, Rinehart and Winston, 1976.

Moos, R.H. *Evaluating Educational Environments.* San Francisco, CA: Josey-Bass, 1979.

Rotter, J.B., J.E. Chance, and E.J. Phares, eds. *Application of Social Learning Theory of Personality.* New York: Holt, Rinehart and Winston, 1972.

Schroder, H.M., M.J. Driver, and S. Streufert. *Human Information Processing.* New York: Holt, Rinehart and Winston, 1967.

Steers, R.M. and W. Porter, eds. *Motivation and Work Behavior.* New York: McGraw-Hill, 1975.

Tyler, L. *Individuality: Human Possibilities and Personal Choice in the Psychological Development of Men and Women.* San Francisco, CA; Josey-Bass, 1978.

Weiner, B. *Theories of Motivation.* Chicago: Markham, 1972.

ASSESSING BEHAVIOR FOR
DIVERSIFIED INSTRUCTIONAL PROGRAMMING

David N. King
Houston Academy of Medicine
Texas Medical Center Library

What is it about learning that is so elusive? Competing theories of learning appear and then fall out of favor with disconcerting regularity. From classical conditioning to information-processing theories — most of us eventually admit that we just do not know enough about the human mind to understand the how's and why's of the learning phenomenon.

But if we have a less than definitive view of what learning involves, we do have some pretty good ideas about manipulating situations and information in ways designed to affect behavior. Behavior is the key to the learning process, and behavioral change is the indicator of successful educational programming.

Of course, behavior does not occur in a vacuum. Behaviors are linked together in groups and tied to all sorts of cognitive, attitudinal, and environmental circumstances. The failure to identify the critical elements in behavior groups or the failure to address the critical elements with appropriate educational intervention, almost always results in failure to effect desirable behavioral changes. (In other words, if we do not identify the right behavior out of a complex group for educational action, or if the educational effort does not adequately address that behavior, learning does not take place.)

The first topic of this paper is to consider a method of assessing behaviors and the causes of those behaviors for planning educational programs. The second topic concerns selecting the behaviors which user education might effectively address.

Educational Diagnosis

Through a process of educational diagnosis developed by Lawrence Green and his colleagues,[1] and since applied with excellent success in the field of health education,[2] we are able to categorize behavior according to factors that contribute to its occurrence and maintenance. These categories of factors are referred to as

FIGURE 1

PRECEDE

Predisposing, Reinforcing, and Enabling Causes
in Educational Diagnosis and Evaluation

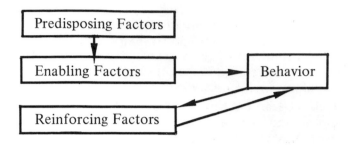

Predisposing Factors: Forces that provide the motivation or rationale for behavior. Included are beliefs, knowledge, values and attitudes that predispose people to act.

Enabling Factors: Attributes, skills, and resources that make it possible for action to occur. Absence of these factors prevents behavior from taking place.

Reinforcing Factors: Factors which provide the incentive for behavior to be maintained. Absence results in a lack of support for behavior to continue.

---

predisposing, enabling, and reinforcing, and form a model that enables us to sort the behaviors for program planning (figure 1).

Predisposing factors are forces that provide the motivation or rationale for behavior. Included in this category are the knowledge, attitudes, beliefs, and values that predispose people to act.

Enabling factors are attributes, skills, and resources that make it possible for action to occur, and conversely, whose absence prevents behavior from occurring.

Reinforcing factors are those which provide incentive for behavior to be maintained. Their absence entails a lack of support for existing behavior to continue.

Let's take a look at an example of an application of educational diagnosis to a user education problem (figure 2). Let's assume that

FIGURE 2

Factors Associated with Graduate History Students
Not Demonstrating Effective Library Skills

Importance Changeability

1. *Predisposing Factors*
   A. Belief that existing library skills are adequate
   B. Overestimation of knowledge of the literature
   C. Feelings that time for effective searches unavailable
   D. Belief that library staff and collections inadequate
   E. Low estimate of value of library skills
      etc.

2. *Enabling Factors*
   A. Library provides no instruction for this group
   B. Department does not provide bibliography course
   C. Lack of effective handouts and guides in History
   D. No effective library-departmental relationships
      etc.

3. *Reinforcing Factors*
   A. Faculty do not stress importance of library skills
   B. Peers do not practice effective library use
   C. University does not require students to develop or
      demonstrate library skills
   D. Faculty do not refer students to librarians
      etc.

----

graduate students in the History Department are not doing a very
good job of library research.

This is just a hypothetical case, but not uncommon. I think we
can see that there are some pretty strong reasons evident, from looking at the predisposing factors, why they are demonstrating inadequate library skills. And, after considering the enabling factors, we
see that there are some critical elements missing which enable students to continue their poor behavior unabated. Of course, there is
not much evidence of incentive to develop good library skills either,
from looking at the reinforcing factors.

Now, the next step in the diagnostic process is to go through and
rate each factor in the list as to its importance.[3] For example, we
would probably decide that predisposing factor A is a principal reason why students are demonstrating poor library skills. The same

would be true for reinforcing factor A. So these two items would be rated high in importance. On the other hand, some of us might consider enabling factor B to be relatively unimportant, if enabling factor A were present. So it might receive a low rating.

The final step in the diagnostic process requires that we go through the list again and rate each factor on the basis of its changeability. If a factor can be easily changed, we would rate it higher than a factor that would be very difficult to change. Thus, enabling factor A might be rated high in importance, but considering the attitudes of faculty, might be rated medium in changeability. But enabling factor C and predisposing factor D might both receive a high changeability rating.

The result of this diagnostic approach to assessing behavior is that it provides a picture of what factors are contributing to the behavior, and also a realistic estimate of the opportunities for educational intervention.

WORKSHEET

Factors Associated with

1. *Predisposing Factors*   Importance Changeability

2. *Enabling Factors*

3. *Reinforcing Factors*

Educational Intervention

I am going to return to the topic of assessing behaviors for educational planning, but I would like to move on for the moment to a related topic. This concerns the selection of the behaviors user education addresses.

In her *Library Trends* article a couple of years ago, Gail Herndon Lawrence posed a question about the goals of user education. Her question was: "Are user education librarians in the business of explaining and defending the library, or are they in the business of encouraging and assuring knowledgeable access to information?"[4] To rephrase the question in behavioral terms, is user education concerned

52

with library-use behavior, or is it concerned with information-handling behavior?

In the past, many librarians felt relatively secure that the distinction made in this question was, for most practical purposes, unnecessary — if not meaningless. Effective use of information required the effective use of libraries. The proliferation of bibliographic instruction programs during the last decade was indicative that the attitude was not entirely unwarranted.

But there are two rather disconcerting items that give me the impression that, so far anyway, user education has been more concerned with teaching library-use rather than with improving the ability of our clientele to use information. The first of these is our almost undeviating disregard for instruction for any purpose other than student research. A few libraries have been successful in providing instruction to faculty, fewer still have offered instruction to secretaries. But how many programs have you heard of that deal with anything other than library-use?

The second item is our persistence in ignoring the admonitions of our information scientists that traditional information networks are changing, and that there is a role for user education in the new information marketplace.[5] But that role is certainly a different one than what we typically think of as library instruction.[6]

We should not delay much longer in making a decision in this matter. We are on the threshold of some truly significant advances in user-friendly computer systems. Perhaps the most impressive to date is the Paperchase system.[7] It is so effective that neophyte users can conduct literature searches quickly and easily, with no training.

The role of instruction in library use certainly will not be affected by all this for quite some time. But I am suggesting that, if we are concerned with educating our clientele in the use of information, as well as in the use of libraries, the opportunities are upon us. A number of medical academic libraries have already begun to diversify their user education programming.

I would like to return now to the program planning approach we used earlier. This time, let's use as an example the development of a program designed to meet the information handling needs of faculty and researchers in the sciences (figure 3). These people rely heavily on their personal knowledge of the literature in their specialties, personal collections of reprints, and professional relationships with their colleagues to meet their information needs.[8] And their use of the literature is usually very effective. But they are often unaware of pertinent literature published in sources outside their specialty journals.[9] More significantly, as their personal reprint files increase in size, they often are unable to retrieve information effectively. As they become increasingly aware of the unmanageability of their

FIGURE 3

Factors Associated with Faculty/Researchers in Sciences
Not Using the Literature Effectively

Importance Changeability

1. *Predisposing Factors*

    A. Overestimation of knowledge of the literature
    B. High value placed on personal and/or
       departmental collections
    C. Low awareness of weaknesses in current
       practices that results in missed literature
    D. Belief that existing library skills are adequate
    E. High value placed on expertise of colleagues
       etc.

2. *Enabling Factors*

    A. Library does not offer instruction related to
       information-use practices of this group
    B. Library does not provide specialized services
       to meet specific information needs
    C. Library does not maintain effective contact
       with department
       etc.

3. *Reinforcing Factors*

    A. Peer relationships support current practices
    B. Relationship with library not sufficiently
       productive
    C. Use of library is often not convenient
       etc.

personal information files, an opportunity is presented for educational intervention.

A half-dozen medical libraries are currently providing instruction in the organization of reprint files as part of their efforts to improve the information-handling ability of their clientele. A number of other innovative or non-typical programs of user education already exist, and more are being developed. Many of these programs are designed to address information-handling behavior rather than library-use behavior. But in many cases, the role of the library in the information network of recipients changes; the library-use behavior of these constituents is improved.

Conclusion

In this paper, I have tried to address two areas that I feel are important in the development of effective user education programs. Both of these are critical to the learning process.

The first dealt with a method of assessing the behavior of clientele in order to plan programs for effective behavioral change. The better our understanding of the factors that contribute to behavior, the better our chance of assuring that learning will occur.

The second dealt with the nature of what it is we want our clientele to learn. The better our grasp of the opportunities for educational intervention into the behavior of our constituencies, the more flexible and creative we are in our educational endeavors, the better our chance of ensuring that our educational programs will meaningfully address the information needs and behavior of our clientele.

Notes

1. Green, Lawrence W., et al. *Health Education Planning: A Diagnostic Approach*. Palo Alto: Mayfield, 1980.

2. Dignan, Mark B. and Patricia A. Carr. *Introduction to Program Planning*. Philadelphia: Lea & Febiger, 1981.

3. A good example of the process appears in: Bonaguro, John A. "PRECEDE for Wellness" *Journal of School Health* 51 (September 1981): 501–506.

4. Lawrence, Gail Herndon. "The Computer as an Instructional Device: New Directions for Library User Education" *Library Trends* no. 1, 29 (Summer 1980): 139–152.

5. Lancaster, F.W. "User Education: The Next Major Thrust in Information Science?" *Journal of Education for Librarianship* no. 1, 11 (1970): 55–63.

6. Lawrence, Gail Herndon, op. cit.

7. Horowitz, Gary L. and Howard L. Bleich. "Paperchase: A Computer Program to Search the Medical Literature" *New England*

Journal of Medicine no. 16, 305 (October 15, 1981): 924–930.

8. There are many pertinent studies. Of significance concerning the information-use habits of health scientists: Strasser, Theresa C. "The Information Needs of Practicing Physicians in Northeastern New York State" *Bulletin of the Medical Library Association* no. 2, 66 (April 1978): 200–209; Murray-Lyon, N. "Communication in Medicine" *Medical Education* 11 (1977): 95–102; Stinson, E. Ray and Dorothy A. Mueller. "Survey of Health Professionals' Information Habits and Needs" *Journal of the American Medical Association* no. 2, 243 (January 11, 1980): 140–143.

9. Again, concerning health scientists: Farmer, Jan and Beth Guillaumin. "Information Needs of Physicians" *Bulletin of the Medical Library Association* no. 1, 67 (January 1979): 53–54.

LIBRARY USE INSTRUCTION
AND THE BASIC LEARNING PROCESSES:
REASONING, WRITING AND RESEARCH

Jon Lindgren
St. Lawrence University

One of the potential hazards to any conference speaker — especially, it seems to me, in the area of librarianship — is that of discussing some topic in such unwholesome quantity of detail as to lapse into the genre of the "how-I-do-it-good" type of presentation. And yet, on the contrary side of the channel to that Scylla lies the Charybdis of vague abstraction, that is, airy discussion of abstract ideas and philosophical principles, with scarcely a glance at the real world. That, too, is a perilous route. Thus, it is a delicate proposition indeed to thread a course between the two extremes of generality and specificity, and so I have chosen today to begin with some general considerations and follow those with some specific examples of application.

Let me begin by throwing out for your inspection what I perceive to be something of a paradox regarding the present state of bibliographic instruction. On the one hand, I seems to me that a great deal remains to be discovered about educating library users, and we are making some substantial progress in advancing those discoveries. At the same time, I detect that we are approaching an impasse regarding our effectiveness in achieving the broader goals we have set for our instructional programs. Let's examine for a moment some of the evidence on both sides of this good news/bad news situation.

First, on the good news side, I assert that we are making some progress. This progress is manifested by the development of our thinking about the areas that lie beyond the teaching of mere mechanics of library use. I think we are clearly becoming less focused — maybe fixated is not too strong a word to describe past practice — on the tools and narrow procedures of library research, that is, use of specific indexes and reference sources. And we are becoming more conscious of our search for a philosophical basis and theory of user instruction, not only a philosophy and theory of library use in research, but also a philosophy and theory of teaching.

Put another way, I think we are coming to distribute our emphasis more evenly between the subject matter of our teaching, the learner, and the instructor. The range of topics addressed by these LOEX conferences over twelve years is one example of that progress. For another, it is almost impossible to imagine such an article as Pamela Kobelski and Mary Reichel's recent one, "Conceptual Frameworks for Bibliographic Instruction,"[1] appearing in the literature, say, ten years ago. Thus, there has been not simply a growth in the quantity of the literature on B.I., but unmistakable development as well.

This may appear all the more significant when we consider that user instruction is a rather new, and relatively unsupported initiative, not just in academe, but even within the library profession, where some are still arguing that we should forget about teaching the user and just answer the questions. As recently as twenty years ago Samuel Rothstein was referring to reference librarianship itself, let alone user instruction, as the "new dimension" of library service.[2] Even ten years ago there was very little reason to attend an ALA annual conference for purposes of professional self-development in the area of user instruction.

This is scarcely the place to review the history of user instruction, but one can indeed generalize a pattern of steady maturation: in the 1950s, orientation tours; in the '60s, practical teaching tips and media instruction on mechanics of use; early '70s, behavioral objectives; mid to late '70s, politics of program building and evaluation of instruction. All of these have been tied to a rather pragmatic, common-sensical, I would even say literal-minded view of the relationship between library resources, the user, and the librarian.

What we are attempting to do in the 1980s, then, is develop further the theoretical principles as they pertain to the user (learning theory), the instructor (teaching theory), and the materials (process theory), and I am confidently hopeful that we are on the proper course.

On the "bad news" side, however, I am frustrated, even troubled by a sense of impasse at several levels of organization.

On the *individual level*: Given what I take to be an ideal setting for user instruction (the BASK program at St. Lawrence University, which I will discuss in some detail), I am seriously disturbed by the frequent inability of some students to assimilate the instruction. Examples from my current teaching: a student doing a major paper on the breakdown of regulatory controls in the Love Canal disaster neglects to search carefully the federal documents. Another student claims not to be able to locate adequate sources to support a paper on the viability of solar heating in the northeast. One can be a philosopher about it and conclude that not every seed that is planted will bear fruit, but these evident failures inevitably cause me to question the durability of any instruction. Perhaps user instruction is doomed to be abysmally inefficient in terms of "long-range" results — here, now, I'm talking "life-long learning," and the like.

At the *community level*: Within the academic community as a whole, I see little evidence that we are making substantial progress against the massive ignorance of faculty and administration regarding the values that inhere in educating library users. Examples: 1) The instructor in a sociology course, "Mass Communications" (populated primarily by freshmen), assigns a student a marvelously imaginative research paper pertaining to the "consumerism aspect of television game shows" — without slightest regard for the student's need to learn how to research this highly sophisticated topic; 2) high-level faculty committees carry on their deliberations without consulting the literature in areas such as curriculum design, evaluation of teaching, retirement benefits, and the like, preferring instead to do their thinking "off the top of their heads," so to speak; 3) composition instructors charge their freshmen to write thoughtful expository essays on the basis of their own limited experience and knowledge, failing to recognize that the resources of the library could extend the students' ability to acquire information and evidence in support of their thinking processes.

At the *society level*: I perceive a failure of the society at large (which includes, of course, the academic community) to understand that in order to realize the broader goals of education, one must learn how to extend one's intellect beyond one's personal resources. In other words, the common-sensical, literal-minded *tabula rasa* theory of education still prevails as the dominant model. It is based on the simplistic concept of education as a body of knowledge to be transferred from master to pupil. Too few people, either inside or outside the education establishment, have grasped the insight expressed by the Omaha junk dealer writing in a recent issue of *The Chronicle of Higher Education*:

> My company took a contract to extract beryllium from a mine in Arizona. I called in several consulting engineers and asked, "Can you furnish a chemical or electrolytic process that can be used at the mine site to refine directly from the ore?" Back came a report saying that I was asking for the impossible — a search of the computer tapes had indicated that no such process existed.
>
> I paid the engineers for their report. Then I hired a student from Stanford University who was home for the summer. He was majoring in Latin American history with a minor in philosophy.
>
> I gave him an airline ticket and a credit card and told

him, "Go to Denver and research the Bureau of Mines archives and locate a chemical process for the recovery of beryllium." He left on Monday. I forgot to tell him that I was sending him for the impossible.

He came back on Friday. He handed me a pack of notes and booklets and said, "Here is the process. It was developed 33 years ago at a government research station at Rolla, Mo." He then continued, "And here also are other processes for the recovery of mica, strontium, columbium, and yttrium, which also exist as residual ores that contain beryllium." After one week of research, he was making sounds like a metallurgical expert.

So the impasse looms large in our attempts to reform education.

Not that there are no reforms going on. Scarcely a day passes that we do not learn of some educational innovation that espouses the goal of achieving computer literacy, from elementary schools through universities.

For example:

—- the April 20, 1982 broadcast of "P.M. Magazine";

—- the current Sunday *New York Times Magazine* ads for "computer camps" (can one imagine exiling one's offspring to "library camps?");

—- the cover story of *Time* for May 3, 1982;

—- and this quotation from *The Chronicle of Higher Education*:

> Computers rapidly are becoming an essential part of the general college curriculum. At several institutions, "computer literacy" is now required for graduation. At many others, computers are being used heavily by students and faculty members in every field of study.
>
> The idea that all students "should be acquainted with the computer in some reasonably respectable fashion is surely no more radical a thought than the proposition that they should be able to read and write," says Stephen White, director of special projects for the Alfred P. Sloan Foundation.

Indulge me for a while as I whine about the easy inroads made by the computer, for I think comparisons and contrasts with the library memory bank can ultimately prove instructive to us.

I'll begin by alluding to an observation made by Abraham Kaplan, who was once a professor of philosophy at another state university about four miles down the road. Kaplan once spoke of the "law of the instrument," which he formulated as follows: "Give a small boy a hammer, and he will find that everything he encounters needs pounding." Those of you who have been enthralled by the computer know exactly how this applies.

As an aside, let me say that I whine about the computer not because I feel that my job is threatened by the incursion of the computer in the library, or in education generally, although I am told that some people do. Nor am I jealous of the computer or envious of its speed and precision.

(I do have some history of jealousy of machines — as an instructor in a college English department, about 60 miles down the road, I used to resent my colleagues in the sciences who had what appeared to me a massive advantage in soliciting the credibility and serious attention of their students insofar as their investigations were inevitably conferred the stamp of authenticity by the physical reality of assorted laboratory equipment, machines, and devices. In the English department, on the other hand, I was doomed to inhabit an invisible world of ideas — oh, sure, we had the printed word in the late 1960s.)

But I digress. The point is not so much that I have a history of jealousy toward machines, but the particular nature of that jealousy which is based on the ease with which it solicits our passive acquiescence. Many people more knowledgable than myself have noticed how the computer and all machines tend to lop off our options and thus impose limitations on us; that is the basis of their alleged dehumanizing influence. Yet everyone can agree that anything that takes over the humdrum mechanical work has quite the opposite of dehumanizing effects. Rather, it releases us from rote work, and frees us to explore our humanity further in new directions. What, then, is my problem with machines — specifically, the computer? My problem is that just as the computer is an instrument to enhance the processes of thinking, communication, and the sharing of information, so is the library. But whereas the computer is able to attract and compel the attention of scholars, educators, students — even the man-on-the-street — the library seems to creep along in its petty pace from day to day locked into its traditional role of respository or warehouse, with much of its potential unacknowledged, unexploited for lack of vision of the possibilities for library literacy. Until we can articulate a fresh vision of library use, we will be inhibited and hampered in our attempts to develop library literacy in our clientele.

Specifically, the old vision of the library is hung up on its emphasis on finding what Patricia Knapp referred to as the "answer to the question" rather than "evidence to be examined," and the computer reinforces overwhelmingly the "answer to the question" approach to library research, not the search for "evidence to be examined."

I know a good many of you are champing at the bit to remind me of the wonderful progress being made in computer applications to the library, "creeping in its petty pace from day to day" indeed! I acknowledge and am grateful for the assistance of the computer (OCLC in my institution) for its contributions to the resource processing and delivery systems. Regarding data bases, I am similarly willing to pay my respects, although here I have much less acquaintance, and I am not going to rehearse for you all the arguments pro and con data base usage in the undergraduate academic library. I'm very sure you know them as well or better than I. I can confidently assert, however, that until data base searching is refined to a state of utter transparency (that is, direct interaction between the mind of the user and the machine ("user friendliness" to the nth degree), there will be something of importance lost if we unwittingly allow the computer to close the door quietly on traditional methods of library research, and on the advances I think are yet to be made in the teaching of those methods. For this reason: the library we now have is in fact a "machine," use of which is capable of much further development towards a state of transparency between the user and all that we label information. That is the mission of user instruction: to secure that capability in our clientele before it atrophies for lack of use.

The latter part of that statement, implying that the computer will in some way diminish our research capability, is bound to arouse considerable dispute, and yet I don't have time today to develop the idea, nor is it an essential argument to resolve for today's purposes. I would, however, like to pick up the first half of the statement and carry it further. To repeat: "The library we now have is in fact a 'machine,' use of which is capable of much further development towards a state of transparency between user and all that we label information, and that is the mission of user instruction."

Let me first say a few words about machines to support the notion that a library is like a machine. You can see, I like machines and I want to identify my work with them. You will notice first that I am using the word "machine" in its broadest almost metaphorical sense. In such a vein we might consider a broom to be a kind of machine. It is a machine which extends the hand's ability to do a specific job called "sweeping." Like all machines, the broom imposes responsibilities, and poses occasional threats, e.g., it requires us to provide a place for it to stay: a broom closet. It may cause us frustration when it wanders off or is mislaid. It may trip us on a darkened stair. It may demand to be cleaned occasionally or at least have its lint picked off, and so on. But overall it is very "user friendly," and its assets far outweigh its liabilities.

If we had the time for it, we could go on and on in like manner noticing how all of our various machines, from simple to complex, serve to extend our senses and sensibilities and our capabilities outward, but always with some element of threat, loss, or limitation:

--- brooms, baseball mitts, fly rods, guns, nuclear warheads — all are machines that extend the hand.

--- eyeglasses, television, microscopes, Voyager — these extend our eyes.

--- megaphones, stereos, radios extend the ears (the SONY Walkman can extend our ears even while we jog).

--- abacuses, calculators, computers, books and libraries extend our ability to think, to remember, and to communicate thought.

Increasingly these days, however, our awe is solicited in favor of the marvels of miniaturization. We are told, for example, that a mini-computer that today sits on a desk top has all the capability of early computers which required massive housing areas. It doesn't stretch the mind too far to imagine that today's Pac-Man machine, back in the days of the vacuum tube, might have occupied half the space of a small library, however dubious the purposes might have been.

And yet, moving the opposite way, why does the "macro" world not stimulate, excite, and challenge our imaginations? Why can't we become as easily infatuated with the idea of tapping the original mind and memory bank of civilization, which is comprised in its libraries? Isn't it pleasurable, as well as intellectually rewarding, to imagine oneself in the library as an electron racing through the electronic system making connections between various thinkers, recorded phenomena, events, experiments, creative and artistic expressions — moving into and through various time periods — geographical and cultural spaces — gobbling up those endless dots of data, recorded experiences, analytical thinking, artistic expressions — in short, "information," like a giant Pac-Man?

If I treat these as more than rhetorical questions, I can come up with some tentative answers. For one, the element of newfangledness is missing with conventional, traditional use of libraries. Another reason is the sheer evanescence of mental experience. It seems more real to dwell in the physical world than in the mental world. Another reason: the human propensity toward mental laziness and passivity. Running a marathon or playing hours of Pac-Man are in a way more passive pursuits than researching an idea in the library. Yet another: the low priority held for information in academia. I won't gloss that one, merely assert that it is true.

Finally, and most importantly to our purposes, I think it is partly true that library users tend to eschew the intellectual pleasures of extending their human potential ("informing" themselves in a couple of senses of the word) because: a) they have little vision of the possibilities; b) there is little tradition urging them toward it; and c) they don't quite understand how. And here, of course, is where instruction in library use comes in. I have occasionally thought that if we could make our instruction reveal the ways to bridge the gap between the individual mind and the mind of civilization, we would find our students as enticed to stretch and exercise their minds in the context of the great and not so great thinkers, researchers, and artists of the past, as they are enticed today toward stretching and exercising their bodies.

So, the library is a machine, and we need to develop and understand our relationships with our machines that we may allow them to extend ourselves to the fullest without enslaving us. In fact, we inevitably do establish relationships with our machines, but we don't always understand fully enough that relationship in order to exploit their potential while sidestepping their pitfalls. For example, I know that nothing worth reading can ever be written with a ballpoint pen; yet, how often do I write with a ballpoint — presumably much less well — simply because it is there? Machines always will re-define us, the more so in positive ways if we can learn how to let them, without surrendering our control and our free will. Let me give you some examples of our relationships with machines:

— psychologically: According to my freshman psychology instructor several years back, a red sports car is a phallic symbol.

— socially: Television is a machine that helps define our sense of reality; it provides us with symbols (e.g., Archie Bunker) and images (e.g., of violence).

— economically: The auto industry dominates our national economy — currently, much to our anguish — especially here in Michigan.

— politically: The bomb confers power and responsibility that we may be immature to exercise capably.

64

—— intellectually: The computer and the library shape our ability to think and our patterns of thinking; they don't merely feed us answers.

Let me emphasize my point: our clients do not understand their relationship with the library machine.

What are some of the detailed functions of the library machine? In addition to the obvious overall memory function, let's look specifically at the reference collection, which has the characteristics of high-speed efficiency in support of using the overall machine. We use the reference collection in several ways:

1) To extend and elucidate our understanding of what we are reading. Indeed, a dictionary is a most obvious kind of machine insofar as it extends our ability to remember and clarify the use of the basic building blocks of abstraction — i.e., words and language.

2) To provide access to, and control over, the other constituent machines: Card catalog, indexes and abstracts, most obviously, but what student ever comes to interact effectively with the quotations dictionary machine, for example?

3) To provide capability for quality control: the evaluation.

4) To provide efficient access to fuel: the supportive data.

Well, I don't want to push this idea beyond usefulness into the realm of absurdity, but I submit that it is useful to think of the library and its component parts as a machine made up of constituent machines.

But we need to establish and work to understand the proper relationship with our machines, and this amounts to interacting with them, not just as parts-changing mechanics working mindlessly, but more in the spirit of Robert Pirsig's *Zen and the Art of Motorcycle Maintenance*. That is, we need to develop ingrained habits of interaction with the machine that is the library, habits that go beyond mechanics of use. Here the comparison cited by Ross LaBaugh in one of Carolyn Kirkendall's recent columns in the *Journal of Academic Librarianship* is instructive:

> Central to the issue of evaluation is the issue of what library skills are. If being able to identify elements on a catalog card, or volume numbers in the *Readers' Guide* are skills, then I suppose it is possible to measure the competency of students participating in library instruction programs.

This would be done in the same way one would measure whether a student knows a foreign language — by testing vocabulary. However, I think that knowing a second language means more than knowing vocabulary and grammar. Similarly, library skills are more than recognizing some significant items in a citation.

The highest state of second language absorption is to develop ability to think in that language, almost without being aware of the language medium, That is the ideal that is comparable to achieving "transparency" between the mind of the individual library user and all those other minds through the age, i.e., the library, need I say? An impossible ideal, to be sure, but one that can be fixed as concrete as a worthwhile goal.

Well, all this is rather long on the abstract, theoretical principles, philosophical/conceptual side of the channel, but is highly relevant to articulating a vision of user instruction. It is a vision that emphasizes

a) reflexive, rather than straightforward thinking;

b) process, rather than procedures;

c) concepts of library use, rather than mechanics; and

d) framing a question, rather than getting the answer to it.

The current *Time* magazine tells us that our ". . . thought processes . . . are subject to the impact of the microchip." The library machine can alter our ways of thinking no less.

The key element in my mind in trying to design instruction that in any way attempts to fulfill that vision centers on the idea that the use of the library is presented from an information-functional point of view. I'm not exactly sure what that phrase means, but I think I recognize it (information-functional user instruction) when I see it. It obviously has to do with "integrated library instruction," as that term is commonly understood. All of this floundering to tell you what it is affords ample evidence that there is a lot of work to be done to understand, hence, implement it better, but let me share some information about the St. Lawrence University Basic Academic Skills (BASK) Program as a specific example of the information-functional approach.

One thing that I will not be talking about in describing the BASK program is learning theory and the kind of work that is being done in the field by people like Cerise. I have tremendous respect

66

for this kind of work and immense good faith that there is a lot to be learned about how people learn and the designing of effective instruction, but I have not had the time or inclination to get involved in that direction. Thus, I do not particularly consider myself to be an effective teacher, and the technique that I will describe will be of little or no interest. It consists simply in brief demonstration followed by workshop experience.

What I am offering in place of learning theory and teaching theory are observations about the nature of what we are trying to teach, the information-related function of what McGregor and McInnis have called library "intermediary resources," which constitute the reference apparatus, and the relationship between the librarian and the student.

Let me begin by saying a few hundred words describing the BASK program at St. Lawrence, specifically the library component.

Library Component of the BASK Program

Objectives

The library component of the BASK program ties together the processes of gaining access to information with the uses of that information in the English 102 (Argumentation) and Philosophy 115 (Reasoning) courses. In grandest terms the objective is to support and extend the student's ability to reason logically and articulate the results of that thinking with clarity and precision; for, to deal effectively with real-life arguments (whether one is assessing or composing them) requires that a student learn how to move beyond her/his personal intellectual resources of memory and thinking ability into the realm of recorded information, by the means of gathering not only factual evidence, but also the various analyses and interpretations of evidence on a question.

In seeking to accomplish this, the library component attempts to teach students some concepts of purposive, systematic use of the bibliographic and reference apparatus of the library as well as instruct them in specific techniques of efficient and comprehensive searching.

Procedure

The initial library session provides an overview of the semester's library work in the form of a demonstration of library resources relevant to the assessment of a specific written argument that has been discussed and written about in Argumentation.

Subsequently, the students are divided into small groups (ideally five to eight students each) which meet weekly in the library over the following weeks. These sessions (see sample syllabus) follow a pattern of brief (20 to 30 minutes) demonstration and discussion on a facet of library research, followed by a short workshop (approximately 30 minutes, often extending longer) in which the concept(s) and procedure(s) are practiced in the context of assigned work for either Argumentation or Reasoning. Worksheets are completed either in the workshop session or outside and handed in the following week.

Individual student conferences with the librarian/instructor are held during the final week of the library component in order to assess the preliminary bibliography for the final Argumentation research paper and remedy any deficiencies.

Coordination

The extent to which the library component of BASK is successful in inculcating in students sophisticated patterns of library use is a function of the degree of coordination achieved between it and the other two components. Otherwise, the library component would tend to be perceived by students as comprising little more than a series of isolated mechanical procedures.

Coordination consists of the use of information sources for purposes of both criticizing and constructing written arguments. For example, the seven-step method of argument assessment used in Reasoning may require use of information sources to: clarify and define the statement of the argument (step 1), criticize the premises underlying the argument (step 5), and introduce other relevant arguments, including counter-arguments (step 6). The coordination with Argumentation involves additionally the use of library resources in service of what we call the scholastic model of constructing an argument: gaining different types of overview perspective on a topic, surveying for significant disputed questions, limiting and shaping the argument in an appropriate way, gaining access to additional evidence (including conflicting evidence and opposing viewpoints) pertaining to an argument, and evaluating the quality of information sources. Put together systematically, these information-seeking procedures contribute substantially to a student's ability to reach a singular synthesis and resolution of the argument presented in their major paper for the argumentation course.

I would like to show you in synopsis some details of a couple of the presentations, the ones on statistics (week three of the spring, 1982, semester — see syllabus, Appendix I) and evaluation of resources (week nine).

Statistics Demonstration (Classroom presentation uses transparencies and worksheet)

What I want to emphasize most is that:

a) the demonstration is relevant to the students' course work in either the Logic or Argumentation courses; in other words a *Post* editorial would be further analyzed and assessed in either (perhaps both) of those courses.

b) the emphasis in the demonstration is on the function of the information, not so much the function of the access tool (e.g., *American Statistics Index*); the particulars of using *ASI* and locating the documents come up later in the workshop session.

c) perhaps most importantly, what one finds in the information sources enlarges and illuminates one's thinking on the matter at hand, leading one to ask further questions in order to probe the evidence pertaining to the original argument. (Did gas prices rise between 1973–1979? How much in real dollars? How was consumption affected? Were there more cars on the road? Do we include motorcycles and buses? Were people getting better mileage? Did lowering the speed limit affect that? Is that a form of "conservation law?" How do we know conservation laws don't work?) This is an example of what I mean by interacting with the reference machine. The worksheet, completed under supervision, provides the students with a format to practice similar work in the context of their own topics of work in the logic and writing courses.

Evaluations of Resources Demonstration (Session uses transparencies)

Here again the demonstration emphasizes the function of information as it provides evidence regarding evaluation of two published books — Alvin Toffler's *Future Shock*, and Charles Reich's *The Greening of America*:

a) book reviews

b) biographical information

c) citation indexing

Well, I have taken too much of your time, so let me wrap things up in a hurry. I can see now that I have not at all succeeded in steering a delicate course between the Charybdis of generality and the Scylla of specificity. Rather, I have bashed head-on against each in turn, and you can judge the results for yourself. But I would urge you to do the same, that is, confront head-on the immense job that remains for us to do in further developing the direct object of our instruction (the students), the indirect object (the research process), and, of course, following the metaphor of English grammar, the subject (ourselves, the instructors).

Specifically, I urge you to:

— Involve yourselves with the intellectual, not just the mechanical processes of working with students, whether individually or in group instruction. They are more than just vessels to be filled, and we owe them more than just answers to questions. We owe them a collegial relationship in their search for evidence to be examined. Examples: One can go further toward teaching students what a reference librarian is for by developing a reference service policy that aims to broaden their understanding of the kinds of assistance that are available, and the difference between good questions and poor ones. Further, we need not feel shy to assess their commitment to the scholarly enterprise, and evaluate their performance thereon.

— Learn more about how students learn, and then go out and solve some instructional problems. Here is one I am currently working on: I am concerned that students learn to exercise range of vision in handling a topic. I'm told all great artists possess range. But how does one best instruct students to consider the broad, abstract concepts that can underlie a topic, such as the idea of "ownership of natural resources" that lies behind the topic of severance taxes? Another one I have been working on is instruction that enables students to recognize, and attempt to overcome, the severe limitations of subject access to books through Library of Congress subject headings.

— Learn how to teach in such a way as to inspire students to hear, and then participate in, the ongoing dialogue among the minds of the centuries, as they explore, sometimes purposefully, sometimes not, but whichever, by their own choice — throughout the library machine.

JON LINDGREN
SPRING, 1982

BASK LIBRARY COMPONENT MODULES

WEEK	TOPIC

WEEK   *TOPIC*

Feb. 8, 9   1. *Overview Sources.* Various types of overview (e.g., historical current trends, interdisciplinary relations, abstract conceptual/theoretical underpinning, survey of previous scholarship, and the like) are shown to be available from a variety of reference sources; these also help to locate significant disputed questions.

Feb. 15, 16   2. *Abstracts.* Students are introduced to the use of abstracting journals (e.g., *Psychological Abstracts*). Abstracts are shown to survey journal literature efficiently, provide ready access to dispute questions and counter-arguments, and reveal varieties of approach in scholarly research.

Feb. 22, 23   3. *Statistics.* Examination of the basic sources of statistical data as they are used to provide evidence in building an argument. Variability of statistical information is seen to be a common problem in verifying premises set forth in an argument.

Mar. 1, 2   4. *Government documents.* Emphasis is on locating disputed questions, congressional hearings, as well as factual (including statistical) information from the gamut of government publications.

Mar. 8, 9   5. *Subject access.* Analysis of a topic will reveal its essential elements — and occasionally secondary elements — which can then be translated into subject headings. A hierarchical ordering of these headings, specific to general, is seen to be most useful in exploiting properly the card catalog.

Mar. 15, 16   6. *Access to bibliographies.* The published work of scholars active in both general and specific fields of research can provide useful bibliographic bases

71

upon which to build. In addition, annotated bibliographies introduce the concept of resource evaluation.

Mar. 29, 30   7. *Indexes.* Emphasis is on the contrast of scholarly with popular periodicals, specialized subject indexing, and the frustration coefficient in using various indexes.

Apr. 5, 6   8. *Reference resources.* The reference collection is explored as a ready source of information useful for a) clarifying meaning; b) criticizing premises; and c) buttressing arguments. An unresolved reference question is shown to become a research question.

Apr. 12, 13   9. *Resource evaluation.* Assumptions about authority, reliability, and validity of library information sources are challenged through several means: book reviews, biographical data and citation indexing.

Apr. 19–23   10. *Individual conferences* (sign-up later). Preliminary bibliographies for the final argumentation paper are due. These will be discussed and critiqued at the conference.

SYSTEMATIC DEVELOPMENT
FOR LIBRARY INSTRUCTION PROGRAMS:
ISSUES OF DESIGN AND CHANGE

Constance A. Mellon
University of Tennessee at Chattanooga

Systematic instructional design, a process adapted from the field of computer technology, is currently receiving wide application in both higher education and industry. A method of gradual, orderly planning and evaluation of instruction, systematic instructional design holds great promise for the planning of library instruction. This technique alone, however, is insufficient for developing an instruction program with real institutional impact. This is because faculty attitude, not instructional excellence, is the real barrier to effective library instruction programs.

This paper describes the process of systematic instructional design, then discusses the faculty attitudes which must be changed before this approach can provide its full potential. Two major theories of change are reviewed and their applications to faculty attitudes about the library are considered. Finally, a case example applying these theories to the development of a library instruction program at one institution is presented. It is hoped that this paper will serve to direct the attention of those responsible for library instruction programs to the issue of faculty attitudes and will help to generate discussion of this issue. For, as Ursula Le Guin points out in her novel, *The Dispossessed*,

> It is of the nature of idea to be communicated: written, spoken, done. The idea is like grass. It craves light, likes crowds, thrives on cross-breeding, grows better for being stepped on.

Systematic Instructional Design

The systematic design of instruction is a process-oriented approach usually called instructional development. This approach, while incorporating and applying a variety of personality and learning theories as well as knowledge of the technology of instruction,

73

has its roots in systems analysis, the theoretical base of computer software design. Systems analysis is generally shown as flow charts or block diagrams, the most basic of which contains four components: input, process, output, and a feedback loop (see figure 1).

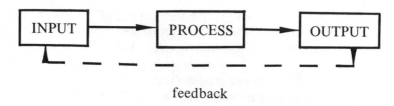

feedback

Figure 1

This basic systems model, applied to the design of instruction, consists of five components: examine, design, develop, implement, and evaluate (see figure 2). In this model the EXAMINE component is the equivalent of input in the systems model, the DESIGN and DEVELOP components equate to process, the IMPLEMENT component is considered as the input stage, and the EVALUATE component provides information to all other stages for feedback and revision.

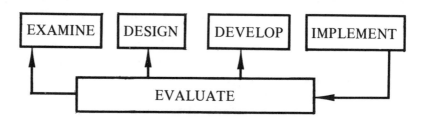

Figure 2

The EXAMINE component, as input, is addressed first. In this stage, five things are considered: students, goals, content, rationale, and assessment. The first, and most important, consideration is the students: Who are they? How are they alike? How do they differ? What entering knowledge can it be assumed they have? A clear examination of the students is vital to the success of a course or an instructional unit. Instruction often fails, not because the design is poor, but because the person designing the instruction did not consider the individual differences among learners or assumed the students had more of a knowledge base than they really did. Librarians see the results of this daily at the reference desk, reflected in such questions as: "How do I find journal articles for a research paper?" "What's a style manual?" or even "Where's the card catalog?"

The next thing to be considered are the goals of the course or instructional unit. Goals address how students should change as a result of the instruction, the knowledge, skills and attitudes they should gain. Once goals are established, content can be addressed. Content considerations include selecting what students must learn or do to create this change and deciding what the minimal content is that all students must know and what content may be optional. Rationale acts as a reality check for both goals and content, requiring an examination of why students should change in the specified direction and how the selected content contributes to this change. Finally assessment determines the acceptable criteria to demonstrate that the students have attained the goals.

The DESIGN component uses the information generated in the EXAMINE stage to create an instructional design. It considers what things should be taught and in what sequence, looking first at an ideal design then evaluating and modifying it to produce a workable trial design. In the DEVELOP stage, objectives are determined for the various parts of the trial design, learning strategies are selected, and materials are prepared and field tested.

In the IMPLEMENT stage, the newly designed course or instructional unit is tried out in the classroom to determine such things as whether the facilities are adequate, what logistical problems may occur, and how materials and activities of the trial design will work in the actual setting. Information from the IMPLEMENT stage is then cycled back during the EVALUATE process to provide the basis for any necessary revisions. As can be seen from figure 2, revisions may be necessary at any of the earlier stages to provide for more effective output. Additional information may need to be gathered, a more realistic or workable instructional design may need to be generated, more or better materials may need to be prepared, or different learning strategies may need to be selected. The importance of such a process to the design of excellent instruction lies in the fact that each area is studied systematically and revision is based on a careful collection, evaluation, and application of data rather than by the arbitrary decision or whim of the instructor.

In higher education, instructional development usually involves at least two people, the professor seeking to redesign a course and an instructional developer whose expertise is in the systematic application of theory and technology to the design of instruction. In this two-part team, the developer is a facilitator while the professor provides the content expertise and makes all final decisions relating to the course or unit of instruction. The value of this approach lies in the interaction between the two participants. The instructional developer, beside providing theoretical and technical knowledge, responds as a naive learner to the instructor as he or she examines the goals, content, and methods specified for the course or instructional unit. The professor, secure in the knowledge that all decisions about the course will be made by him or her, is able to view the goals, content, and method through the eyes of the naive student.

While the instructional development process functions best as an interaction between developer and instructor, it is still useful for anyone developing instruction to approach the design in a systematic fashion, carefully examining the elements comprising the learning situation before determining any strategies and preparing any materials, then evaluating the results before revising. It should certainly be an effective way for the instructional librarian to design and prepare library orientation classes for students. Not only the approach itself, but the theories and technologies associated with its use, provide an excellent base for the improvement of library instruction.

Systematic Design Is Not Enough

As Coordinator of Library Instruction, it was this approach that I used when I began designing the program at my institution, the University of Tennessee at Chattanooga. With five years experience in instructional development, a solid grounding in learning theory and developmental theory, a better than average grasp of the technology of instruction, and the full cooperation and expertise of our reference staff, I went to work to design the best possible classes I could. The students seemed to like them and the professors who requested instruction returned with new classes yet, at the end of the year, we were aware that the program was not making the impact for which we had hoped. Why, I wondered, were the students not incorporating the things they learned into their regular approach to the library? We had broken things down into search strategies, had designed materials incorporating developmental and learning theory, and had provided simple, carefully constructed guides to reinforce what had been learned in the classroom. Yet monitoring the questions at the reference desk seemed to indicate that in many instances only the surface had been scratched. We had succeeded in raising the awareness of the students about the function of the reference librarians and, in many instances, had provided them with a working knowledge of specific tools. But this knowledge seemed to have no generic impact. Students who received library instruction in one course seemed unable to apply the techniques they had learned to other courses or even to other assignments within one course. I remember one English composition teacher complaining,

> You told them that the *Readers' Guide* was not the best resource for most college research. I know you told them. I was there. I heard you. But when the research papers were turned in, most of them had used such magazines as *McCalls, Ladies Home Journal*, and the *Reader's Digest*. Telling them once is just not enough.

Library Instruction As a Stepchild of the College Curriculum

In the words of this composition teacher, I finally decided, was the key to what was wrong with the program. Although "telling them once is just not enough," we have no authority to do otherwise. Designing library instruction is not the same as designing other college instruction since library instruction does not have the same place in the academic curriculum as other college instruction. Librarians who design and deliver this instruction have, for the most part, no control over its placement within the course for which it is requested nor the amount of time allotted to it. Indeed, library instruction is a stepchild of the college curriculum, existing on the beneficence of the teaching faculty.

This provides some interesting contrasts between regular college instruction and library instruction, contrasts which must be considered if the plan is to design a library instruction program with institutional impact. First, regular college instruction has curriculum legitimacy; it exists as courses within academic departments. Library instruction, for the most part, is peripheral to the curriculum, existing as a service at the request of the teaching faculty. Second, regular college instruction involves primary student contact; the students have enrolled in these courses. Library instruction is secondary student contact; the students are not "our" students. Third, regular college instruction involves continuing student contact over a period of a semester or a quarter. Library instruction is usually a single session experience. Fourth, regular college instruction implies control of the reward system; the professor decides how and for what students will be graded. Library instruction usually has no direct relationship to the grade and, even when it does, that is controlled and monitored by the faculty member in charge of the course. In summary, the fact is this. Little or no power for impact upon the student resides in the library faculty responsible for the design and delivery of library instruction.

To obtain the power necessary to provide a library instruction program with lasting student impact, librarians must team with teaching faculty to design and deliver library instruction integrated into the structure of existing courses. The best instructional design in the world, incorporating all of the newest techniques and technologies, cannot possibly have the desired and continuing curriculum impact without the understanding, acceptance, and advocacy of the teaching faculty. Yet here, clearly, we encounter a problem. Faculty themselves are not convinced that librarianship is a "real discipline." Libraries have been part of their lives from the earliest days: story hour at the public library; going with the teacher to the high school library to look for magazine articles in the *Abridged Readers' Guide*; using the tools of their own field to complete their doctoral research. The library is so familiar to faculty that they assume they can use it as well as any librarian. It does not occur to them that there is a good deal they do not know, in fact cannot be expected to know, about using the library.

We can each call up vignettes from our own experience to verify this impression: The part-time instructor who requested a library session, then, when he arrived ten minutes late with his class, waved his hand and declared, "Go ahead. Tell my students what they need to know to use the library. But please don't take any longer than twenty minutes. I have some important things to cover when you're finished." Or the full professor who went to see the director of the library to ask him how to use the ERIC system. "I don't want the reference librarians to know I can't use it," he said. Or finally, the assistant professor completing her doctoral studies who called one Friday and demanded a class for 8 a.m. the following Monday. When informed that more lead time was required, she complained, "But I have to go to the university on Monday about my dissertation and the department chairman told me I could just send my class to the library."

Our first problem, then, is not so much the best way to teach students to use the library; it is rather to change the attitudes of the faculty toward the library, for students reflect the attitudes of their professors. As Raymond McInnis (1978) has declared,

> More than any other factor, the value the classroom instructor attaches to library research determines the students' interest in the use of library materials.

The change necessary in faculty attitude is a subtle one since, while many professors give lip service to the importance of the library in the education of the student, few will be aware of the need to work with a professional librarian in redesigning their courses to include an effective library component. Yet, from the standpoint of legitimizing library instruction and allowing it to have impact upon the students equal to other parts of the curriculum, it is necessary to begin integrating the training and testing of library research skills into the course content of existing classes. To accomplish this task, we must begin by raising faculty awareness of the complexities of academic library use and the value of a course-integrated approach in teaching students to become effective library users. This requires a somewhat different theoretical concentration than the design of instruction since our goal here is more closely related to educational change than to instructional excellence.

Applying Change Theory to the Planning of Library
Instruction Programs

Two change models in particular can provide some direction to the planning of library instruction programs, the educational change model of Ronald Havelock and the innovation adoption model of Everett Rogers. Havelock, in his book on educational change, proposes six stages in the movement of education situations from the way they exist to the way one would like them to be. Three of these stages are useful to the instruction librarian as he or she addresses the issue of how to build an effective program (Havelock, 1973). These stages can be summarized as follows:

1. *Building a Relationship.* A successful relationship between the change agent and his clients, the people he is trying to help, is the key to successful planned change. This depends heavily upon the change agent's personality and skill and how clearly he or she has come to know the client.

2. *Gaining Acceptance.* It is the job of the change agent to convince the people he is trying to help to accept the educational innovation. The activities of the change agent at this stage include promoting awareness of the innovation, explaining, demonstrating and training people in its application to the situation, and integrating the innovation into day-to-day use.

3. *Stabilizing the Innovation and Generating Self-Renewal.* The relevant activities from this stage are internalizing the innovation to insure long term continuation and building

79

competence within the client system to continue the use of the innovation.

Everett Rogers (1971), who developed the most widely known model of change, has provided a five-stage model of how individuals come to adopt an innovation. These stages are:

1. *Awareness stage*. The individual learns of the existence of the new idea but lacks the information about it.

2. *Interest stage*. The individual develops interest in the innovation and seeks additional information about it.

3. *Evaluation stage*. The individual makes mental application of the new idea to his present and anticipated future situation and decides whether or not to try it.

4. *Trial stage*. The individual actually applies the new idea on a small scale in order to determine its utility in his own situation.

5. *Adoption stage*. The individual uses the new idea continuously on a full scale.

In applying these models to the development of a library instruction program, the first consideration should be building a relationship between the instructional librarian and the faculty member. Often the vehicle for this is the existing course-related instruction. Some simple techniques which may prove effective are questioning the faculty as to the goals of the library instruction , designing the instruction to suit the needs of the students as they complete library assignments, inviting faculty to cooperate in teaching library classes, and designing library classes to instruct the faculty as well as their students. Written class evaluations are also a valuable tool for changing faculty attitudes. When faculty have evidence that students feel library classes cover too much materials in too little time, that students would like more library sessions, or that practice of the skills discussed is desired by a majority of students, they become more open to the interaction with librarians' need to integrate an effective library component into course content. Written evaluations also provide the opportunity for faculty-library dialogue on student problems with library use. This can allow the instruction librarian to acquaint the faculty member with library problems from the perspective of the reference desk and to encourage the integration of library assignments into the course content associated with the student's grade.

On an institution-wide basis, the five stage model proposed by Rogers and subsumed under Havelock's stages of Gaining Acceptance and Stabilizing the Innovation, provides some guidance to the instruction librarian on how course-integrated library instruction might be disseminated to the faculty as a whole. Faculty members must be made aware of the possibility of course-integrated library instruction and of the assistance of the instruction librarian in designing such instruction. Some faculty members will decide to try it in their own courses. Where it is successful, adoption will occur.

An important factor in the application of these models is embodied in the words "planned change." Planned change is a slow process with each step carefully thought out. It is important for the instruction librarian to carefully plan program goals, both long-term and short range, to determine how to best achieve these goals and who might facilitate their attainment. If the long-term institutional goal is course-integrated library instruction at all levels, where should the first focus be placed? Should efforts be concentrated on certain faculty who seem influential with their colleagues or on a specific area with some possibility of success? If concentration is on a specific area, who are the opinion leaders in that area? How can they be persuaded to integrate library instruction into their courses? What can the instruction librarian do to assure that integration will be successful? Furthermore, these issues need to be considered continually throughout program development since people and priorities rarely remain static over an extended period of time. The change process and those attempting change must be flexible and adaptable if the desired change is to be effectively accomplished.

This provides a brief overview of some change models and how they might be applied to the development of an effective library instruction program. To see how planned change might operate in relation to library instruction, the first phase of a comprehensive long-range program currently being implemented at the University of Tennessee at Chattanooga will be described.

A Case Example of Planned Change

In March, 1980, the library of the University of Tennessee at Chattanooga, with funding from the Lyndhurst Foundation, began a five year project to provide library instruction to students wherever appropriate across the curriculum. During the first semester of the academic year 1980–81, needs assessment data was collected through testing, interview, observation, and classroom contact with over sixteen hundred students from freshman to graduate level. From these data, it was decided that, in order to provide a consistent base

81

of library skills, integrating a library component into the freshman composition courses would be the initial focus of the newly developing program.

Building on the basis of a year long working relationship with the Director of Composition, a three year plan was developed. According to this plan, materials were developed by the Coordinator of Library Instruction. These materials outlined a recommended library research process and provided sample units of instruction. These materials were reviewed by the Director of Composition and used during one academic year in the library's current course-related instruction program. The materials are the basis for an upcoming summer development project.

The staff for the summer development project includes the Director of Composition, the Coordinator of Library Instruction, and a reference staff member, all of whom are available to the project on their regular twelve-appointments. In addition, funds have been made available to hire four faculty members, two from the English Department's Composition Committee, one from the humanities and one from the sciences. Under the direction of the Coordinator of Library Instruction and using the sample materials which were developed, this group will work together to prepare an entry level research component for English 102. Since it is the role of English 102 to prepare students for more advanced research in other college courses, the proposed project staff includes both English 102 faculty members and faculty members representing other college disciplines. The library reference staff will provide library expertise as needed during the course of the project. The outcome of the summer development project will be an agreed-upon basic research method and instructional materials and techniques by which this method will be taught in the English 102 classes.

Early in the fall of 1982, Update Sessions will be held to acquaint all English 102 faculty with the processes, materials and techniques developed during the summer. Faculty will be asked to try the instructional materials and to discuss how they might be used in their English 102 classes during the coming academic year.

In both semesters of the 1982–83 academic year, the instructional sequence will be implemented in as many sections of English 102 as is feasible and its effectiveness evaluated. The evaluation will be directed by the English Department's Composition Committee and the results will provide part of the basis for materials revision by the original project staff during the following summer.

Meanwhile, during the academic year 1982–83, an interdisciplinary committee of six faculty will be formed consisting of representatives from each of the schools that comprise the university. This committee will be given released time to survey their schools as to current library assignments given in existing courses and the goals of these assignments. The first week of the summer term 1983, this committee will review the survey results and determine its implications for the English 102 library component. Part of this process will include each committee member evaluating and planning the revision of a library assignment from his or her own course. The information from this review process will be provided to the original project staff for use in their summer revision process.

During the last academic year of the project, all involved participants will be asked to review and comment on the materials, with any further revision being completed by the summer of 1984. At this point, materials should be in final format and can be printed for sale through the bookstore. This would complete the integration of library instruction into the English 102 course.

In Summary

Systematic instructional design has been described as a process wherein a faculty member and an instructional developer work together to examine, design, develop, implement and evaluate a course or unit of instruction. This method, while useful in improving the quality of instruction, is insufficient by itself to provide enough consistent training for students in library strategies, tools, and techniques. To accomplish this, library instruction must be integrated into the structure of existing courses. Access to existing courses, however, is under the control of teaching faculty, many of whom have a simplistic view of the library and feel that their students already use it easily and effectively. Changing these attitudes must be the first focus of a library instruction program aimed at institutional impact. Through examining and applying theories of change to program planning, instruction librarians may be better able to move toward program goals in a systematic, gradual and continual way.

References

Havelock, R.G. *The Change Agent's Guide to Innovation in Education*. Englewood Cliffs, NJ: Educational Technology Publications, 1973.

McInnis, R.G. *New Perspectives for Reference Service in Academic Libraries*. Westport, CT: Greenwood Press, 1978.

Rogers, E.M. with Shoemaker, F.F. *Communication of Innovations: A Cross-Cultural Approach*. 2d ed. New York: The Free Press, 1971.

B.I. IN BRITAIN:
COMP 102, WHERE ARE YOU?

Constance P. Mulligan
Northern Kentucky University

To quote a line from Lewis Carroll, one of the most famous dons to ever grace the hallowed halls of Oxford University, this is "A tale begun in other days, When summer suns were glowing."[1] In 1981, I was fortunate enough to travel to Britain where I participated in the Second International Conference on Library User Education held at Keble College, Oxford. Realizing the opportunity of the moment, I made plans to remain in Britain for a few weeks of post-conference travel. During this time, I was able to visit several universities, colleges and polytechnics which were noted for their keen interest in user education, aided by a faculty project grant from my home institution, Northern Kentucky University. Through the advice of Ian Malley, the Information Officer for User Education in Britain and Frank Gibbons, a friend and senior lecturer in the Department of Library and Information Studies at Liverpool Polytechnic, I was able to contact resource people involved with bibliographic instruction in select institutions prior to my arrival to make suitable arrangements. And thus, I was off on my biblio-odyssey of Britain!

Before I proceed with my travels, however, I feel a brief explanation of what the British call their "tertiary educational system" might be in order, for I needed explanation several times along the way. As Peter Fox pointed out in his introductory article presented at the First International Conference on Library User Education, there are rigid distinctions between universities, polytechnics and colleges in Great Britain.[2] Of course, Oxford and Cambridge are, as to be expected, much in a class by themselves. In the Oxbridge tradition, students maintain a close working relationship with a single tutor, leaving the librarian with little role in the imparting of information skills. The red-brick or civic universities are usually several decades old and are so-called because they are based in major cities. The polytechnics, which were upgraded to university status in the sixties, have a more practical and vocational bent and are a driving force behind user education in Britain, as are many of the smaller colleges of further and higher education. During my tour, I had the opportunity to visit libraries representing each of these different institutions and although methodologies varied, I soon recognized a common element in the user education programs.

> It takes all the running you can do,
> to keep in the same place.
> If you want to get somewhere else,
> you must run at least twice as fast as that.[3]

With this admonition from Carroll's Red Queen in mind, I boarded the BritRail in Oxford heading towards the Loughborough Institute of Technology's Pilkington Library — a fitting beginning for a study of user education in Britain. Loughborough is the home site for not only Ian Malley, whom I have already recognized as the Information Officer for User Education in Britain, but the Library Instructional Materials Bank, a diversified collection of materials on user education and *Infuse*, a periodical devoted to user education activities. Here, Bob Rhodes, head of the library's Information Office, informed me that a good sixty to seventy-five percent of the librarians in the information section (what we in the States would call a reference department) were actively involved in library user education. Their particular program placed a heavy emphasis on intruction for engineering students — civil, electrical, mechanical, and chemical — as well as instruction in such areas as physics and animal and plant ecology. As Rhodes pointed out, user education at Loughborough was predominantly oriented toward the sciences and engineering which, in Britain, has been the rule and not the exception as I soon discovered.

From Loughborough, I visited the University of Nottingham's Science Library, where I was pleased to find an active interest in user education from all vantage points — librarians, teaching faculty and administration. Geoffrey Hayhurst, head of the Science Library, explained that subject librarians oversee all user education activities for all students in their particular subject area, acting as a liaison not only for students in that discipline but for faculty as well. Through this method, a librarian is not only conversant with the vocabulary of a discipline but also knows the literature, engendering a professional camaraderie and confidence between students/faculty and librarian. Although a time-consuming order for a subject librarian with other responsibilities as well, this seemed a fine example of sound British logic. In fact, this particular method of conducting library user education seemed the perfect solution to one who had been struggling to provide effective instruction to science majors armed with a humanities background. Hayhurst pointed out that there was some "induction" (British orientation) work done, but that the great majority of instruction was aimed at students in their second or third year. At this time, students would be starting individual project work requiring use of abstracting and indexing sources — built-in motivation for library instruction. Visiting the Main Library at Nottingham, I found the same methodology employed: several subject librarians, in addition to one general reference librarian, providing instruction. As I deduced from my visits, the general reference librarian, that staple of public services in the U.S. academic libraries, proved to be a rare bird in the British academic setting, as was the general reference or "enquiry" desk.

From Nottingham, I ventured cross-country to Edinburgh, my base for visiting Stirling University in Stirling, Scotland. Here, Hilary Duggua, Science Librarian, provided me with a first hand look at one of the more innovative cooperative endeavors in British user education, the Travelling Workshop Experiment. For those not familiar with the TWE, let me briefly summarize this successful venture which is currently being used in many user education programs throughout Britain and has even immigrated to several programs in the States. The Travelling Workshop Experiment, a research project funded by the British Library Research and Development Department, originated in 1974 at Newcastle Polytechnic Library and was designed to provide self-instructional materials describing information sources in a particular subject in comprehensive, self-contained packages. Working with general supervision from a librarian, students learn at their own pace through a variety of media — reading, listening to tapes, viewing slide/tape (or tape/slide as our British friends say) programs, examining bibliographic tools and using them to complete practical exercises.[4] Stirling University was a test site for use of the TWE Biological Information package. There, workshop sessions were videotaped chronicling student and librarian reaction to and interaction with the various information presented. As an instructional tool, the package proved successful with librarians, students and faculty, due not only to its highly specialized subject orientation but also to the self-motivated approach used. Stirling's library uses the TWE Social Welfare and British History packages as well in their instruction program.

Once again, the instruction program at Stirling was slanted towards the needs of users in their own subject area. In fact, there was even library instruction for students in the aquaculture program, a discipline concerning fish farming and fish pathology — certainly one of the more esoteric classes I encountered. Stirling University Library proved unique in other ways as well, with its own Stirling

University Classification System and a Press Room which enabled students of literature, bibliography and librarianship to practice for themselves the main techniques of printing which were employed in the hand press period. Stirling also used a microfiche catalog which, through the convenient format, was made available on each floor of the library. Although not unique in British libraries, this was the first I had seen in my visits.

From Stirling, I travelled again to England, where my next stop was Sheffield University — one of the red-brick variety mentioned earlier — where librarians David Jones and Susan Frank were both patient and informative in their explanations of British user education and the British library system in general. Blessed with not only a seminar room which was aesthetic and utilitarian but a resident graphic designer as well, the librarians used lecture and workshop sessions combined with guided question papers to provide library instruction for students in disciplines ranging from geology to genetics. Librarians here had also been successful with course integrated instruction in select post-graduate programs.

Again noting the highly specialized subject bent of the instruction offered and recalling the scarcity of instruction offered in the arts and humanities at other institutions, I began to piece together some general assumptions about British user education I had made along the way. With the helpful guidance of David Jones, I came to understand how the British curriculum in itself is very much a deciding factor in the slant of user education. As Jones explained, after some congenial prodding, there is no equivalent in the British curriculum of a Composition 102, much less 101, course — those firmly ensconced standards of American collegiate education.

This absence of what seems, to U.S. librarians, to be a mainstay of the U.S. academic curriculum is due to several factors. As Peter Fox noted in his aforementioned paper, only fourteen percent of the university age population actually attend in Britain as compared to around fifty percent in the U.S. This small percentage combined with the highly selective system in Britain and the well-known pecking order among institutions produces a much smaller range of ability among students in British higher education.[5] Too, because of the selective nature of even secondary education in Great Britain, students entering a university, college or polytechnic are already aimed at study in a particular discipline — ready-made homogeneous groups ripe for instruction. One need only compare this to the much wider range of ability among students in the U.S. to appreciate the advantage. Thus, librarians engaged in user education in Britain are able, by means of the educational system itself, to engage in a much more subject-oriented instruction program than those of us in the U.S. who are often still struggling to provide the rudiments of term-paper research.

Armed with this explanation, I was anxious to see if this subject orientation was used in the polytechnics. At Preston Polytechnic Library, I discovered what I felt to be one of the best examples of user education geared toward subject disciplines. Escorted by Allan Foster, Deputy Librarian at Preston, I soon learned that the enthusiasm for and emphasis on library instruction found in polytechnics spring not only from the librarians themselves but from Britain's Council for National Academic Awards. In polytechnics, degree courses have to be approved by the Council, whose subject expert panels often require that a certain portion of the coursework be devoted to library instruction.[6] Thus, subject librarians at Preston and other polytechnics have the welcome, but rare, opportunity of being involved with new course planning. In fact, as Malcolm Stevenson pointed out in his article entitled "Education of Users of Libraries and Information Services," in polytechnic libraries, subject and professional qualifications of the librarian are quite often put before teaching expertise and personal qualifications when deciding who should be involved in the instruction process.[7]

At Preston, subject librarians in business and management, the social sciences, art and design and science and technology provided students with detailed instruction in their subject specialties, equipped with five teaching rooms wired for video, demonstration facilities for literature searching and elaborate graphic and photographic services. These latter services were responsible for the production of extremely attractive, clever handouts which were used in lectures and in point-of-use instruction. Preston's library also housed quite an unusual collection of printed and three-dimensional ephemera — including a beautiful collection of English candy tins and old British advertisements, all accessible through a catalog. There was also one of the more amusing see references I've seen in my career:

Clousseau, Inspector. See   Peter Sellers!

The last stop on my excursion was Brunel University, located exactly twenty-eight tube stops on the Piccadilly Line from London proper. Brunel was named after Isambard Kingdom Brunel, the Englishman who designed the largest single-span road bridge in the world. Here, Deputy Librarian R.W.P. Wyatt and Assistant Librarian Liz Chapman took primary responsibilities for instruction, aided by additional subject librarians and a well-executed "induction" videotape starring Ms. Chapman. The shelving system at Brunel, like the user education, was very much subject oriented with all print and non-print materials shelved together in designated areas. In between a glass of dark ale and a cup of tea, I learned that the emphasis on science and engineering that pervaded British user education dated all the way back to 1948. In this year, the Royal Society Conference on Scientific Information brought to light the fact that trained scientists had difficulty using the literature of their particular field, so the need for instruction on utilization of these resources was recognized. Since this time, there has obviously emerged in Britain a conscientious co-operative effort to supply this type of very specialized instruction through organization on a national level. Support of such projects as the Travelling Workshop Experiment, the Library Instructional Materials Bank and the Standing Conference on National and University Libraries' tape/slide scheme[8] has further exhibited the commitment to library user education. Ian Malley has even taken steps toward improving the relevance of library instruction materials by encouraging academic staff in higher education to draw from the LIMB materials in their own subject discipline for purposes of assessing relevance.[9]

Before summarizing my remarks, I would like to recognize those libraries visited which have yet to be mentioned. As I commented quite often along the way, the much heralded Southern hospitality to which I have been accustomed surely found a rival in Britain's own special brand of reception. The additional libraries include Liverpool Institute of Higher Education, where I discovered the Bliss Classification System; Liverpool Polytechnic Faculty of Art and Design, which holds among its claims to fame a former student by the name of John Lennon and the intriguing Captain Liddell Hart collection of fashion, costume and corsets; Mabel Fletcher Technical College, where students designed the costumes used on the BBC Shakespeare series in their theatre wardrobe design course; and Edgehill College of Higher Education, outside of Liverpool, which was experimenting with the use of microcomputers in library instruction. I had also planned to visit the University of Cardiff in Wales, but a failure to change trains at a crucial junction left me eating clotted cream and scones somewhere in Devonshire!

Despite the common problems of staffing, funding, scheduling or "timetabling" as the British say, and lack of support from administration and faculty which we all share, whether in Britain or in the U.S., through my visits I sensed an overwhelming dedication to and belief in library user education as a very integral part of the overall learning process in Britain. To close, I would like to "pinch" a joke told by Peter Taylor in his very entertaining closing remarks at the Conference:

> Why is library instruction like Christopher Columbus? When he started, he didn't know where he was going. When he got there, he didn't know where he was. And he did it all on state monies!

As we all seek directions in our user education programs, a recognition of the library instruction activities in Britain may serve as inspiration and incentive in our own instruction work.

Notes

1. Lewis Carroll, *The Complete Works of Lewis Carroll*, The Modern Library (New York: Random House, 1936), p135.

2. *Library User Education: Are New Approaches Needed? Proceedings of a Conference, Trinity College, Cambridge, 1979.* (London: British Library, 1980), p3.

3. Carroll, p166.

4. *Library User Education* . . . op. cit., p46.

5. Ibid., p5.

6. Charles Crossley, "Progress and Recent Developments in British Libraries," in *Progress in Educating the Library User*, ed. by John Lubans, Jr. (New York: R.R. Bowker Co., 1978), p155.

7. Malcolm Stevenson, "Education of Users of Libraries and Information Services," *Journal of Documentation* 33 (March 1977): 62–63.

8. *Library User Education* . . . op. cit., p46.

9. Ian Malley, "LIMB," *Aslib Proceedings* no. 7, 30 (July 1978): 273.

THE INTERNATIONAL STUDENT
IN YOUR LIBRARY: COPING WITH
CULTURAL AND LANGUAGE BARRIERS

Sally Wayman
Pennsylvania State University

Those librarians who work on public service desks have no doubt noticed the increasing numbers of Oriental, Asian, Latin and African students needing assistance in using the library. According to the Committee for Foreign Students and International Policy, an arm of the American Council on Education, their numbers will swell from the present 312,000 to over a million in the early 1990's. Within a decade, ten percent of all American college enrollment could be international students. Richard Berendzen, Chairman of the Committee and President of American University, predicts that "by the 1990's, the presence of foreign students could be one of the most powerful themes in American higher education."[1]

At the Pennsylvania State University Libraries, encounters with international students have been, for the most part, pleasant and satisfying. However, some incidents cause concern: the African student who cajoled a student shelver into looking up his books; the Middle Eastern student who called a librarian a "liar" when she informed him we didn't own a book he needed; the Chinese student who left bewildered because she was too polite to say she didn't understand our instructions on the card catalog. Situations like these cause frustration and misunderstanding for both librarian and patron; such tensions can lead to permanent anxieties which can affect the nature and impact of instructional services.

At one time, foreign students studying in America were from European countries with cultures somewhat similar to ours. Today's students are coming from Third World, or developing nations, in growing numbers. At Penn State, two thirds of our foreign students are from the Third World.[2] Students from these cultures must cope not only with language differences, but with religious, societal, familial, and educational dissimilarities. Adjustment to the American educational process is one of the most severe. Several variables influence the interactions between international students and the teacher or librarian, and help determine the effectiveness of adaptation to our system of education. Three of these are: communication; learning styles, attitudes and behaviors; and expectations and previous experience in libraries. These variables can be the sources of conflict when two different cultures meet in any educational setting, including libraries.

For years, librarians have studied the special needs of the handicapped, the disadvantaged, the elderly, and minority groups, but we have not yet begun to examine the unique problems of the international student on our campuses. This paper will, using the three variables of conflict, attempt to identify these problems, why they occur, and offer some suggestions to remedy them.

Communication

While working with international students, the most obvious differences we encounter is that of communication — oral, written, non-verbal. Surveys have found that foreign students regard this as the most pressing problem they have in adjusting to American education.[3] The problem is compounded because few Americans speak any language but English, and Americans are generally insensitive to cultural differences in the communication process. Dr. Merton J. Kahne, psychiatrist at MIT and counselor to many foreign students, feels "it is precisely our unfamiliarity with any but our own cultural cues that is largely responsible for the repetitive difficulties that international students find themselves in and for which they are obliged to bear full responsibility."[4] A Nigerian student comments, "it seems that Americans expect everybody to speak like Americans and are impatient if one does otherwise."[5]

International students have the most difficulty with English in the classroom, a significant problem when many teachers consider class participation to be part of a student's grade.[6] While an Asian's reading speed is one half that of the average American student, his oral comprehension is often slower in the same ratio.[7] English language courses still stress reading and grammar, rather than oral communication, and any oral emphasis may be on British accent and style. American teachers, librarians, and students do not use standard English, but use local accents and intersperse their lectures with slang. Most lectures are delivered too rapidly, and instructors rarely write standard terms on the board. The TOEFL exam (Teaching of English as a Foreign Language) used to measure students' capabilities in English, is indicative only of written skills and tends to compare his knowledge of English with that of other foreign students. A Norwegian student once wrote, "Help me. I speak beautiful English but I do not understand it."[8]

There are other cultural differences which affect communication.

As a librarian, your sex may influence the way an international student approaches you. A Middle Eastern student, raised in a culture where women are not as important or educated as men, may not always respect or even believe the advice of a female librarian. On the other hand, students from Latin American cultures, which are maternally dominant, may readily follow the female librarian's word.

Americans are often oblivious to the social status of foreign nationals. Many Africans have aristocratic and noble heritages, and may insist on a reasonable amount of deference. This may be interpreted as offensive or obnoxious behavior. Some students, conscious of stratified societies, do not trust the word of a secretary and may insist on appealing to a higher authority — sometimes more than one. A librarian at an information desk may be perceived as a lowly subordinate, and be bypassed. Many cultures only recognize titled peoples' needs. One of Penn State's International Student office directors found that in order to get service at African embassies, he must identify himself as Dr. ————, Director of ———— . Otherwise, he never gets to speak to the appropriate personnel.

Body language is a type of non-verbal communication. A female librarian who looks an Arabic man in the eye may be perceived as defiant or guilty of too much familiarity, while all she wants to be is attentive. While Americans see a firm handshake as a sign of confidence, the Arab sees it as disrespectful. Westerners nod their heads up and down to mean yes, or a positive signal. In some cultures this is a negative signal. A student orally telling a librarian that he understands how to find the stacks while nodding his head, may actually be saying something very different with his body. How we stand, walk, or gesture, or even the physical distance we leave between ourselves and others, may be taken as having meanings we never intended when communicating with those from other cultures.

Americans have not yet learned to be sensitive to these communicative differences. Think of the Arabic student who needs to find a book with the call number LB705 .6 .B2. In his language, the numeral 7 stands for six, the 0 represents five, the period is a sign for zero, and he uses a completely different alphabet. Under stress, he may have trouble with the translation. Remember also the plaintive remarks of one foreign student: "I think in Thai, I am fluent in Japanese, I read French, and I cry in English."[9]

Learning Styles, Attitudes, Behaviors

In library user education, the librarian acts as a teacher, instructing either one-to-one or in a classroom situation. In both these settings, the librarian's job is to facilitate learning. Each individual has preferred ways of organizing what he or she sees, hears, remembers, and thinks about. These we call modes or styles of learning, and these preferences can be unique and specific to a cultural group. Simply put, not every nationality learns alike.

In 1974, the United States Supreme Court decided the case of Lau vs. Nichols, in which the plaintiff charged that Chinese children were not receiving the same benefits as white children from a California school system. In deciding for the plaintiff, Justice William O. Douglas wrote:

> Every student brings to the starting line of his educational career difference advantages and disadvantages caused in part by social, economic, and cultural background, created and continued completely apart from any contribution from the school system.[10]

These modes of learning result from both the child's cultural milieu and the teaching style of the parents.

Societal child rearing practices play a large role in determining an individual's learning style. In America, mothers use questioning as a teaching strategy, i.e., "What's the flower's name?" or "Isn't the kitten soft?" There is much verbal interchange between parent and child, and recitation of events is expected, i.e., "What did you see at the circus?" In foreign cultures, a child learns by observation and imitation. A Japanese child may go fishing with his grandfather many times, during which he observes how his grandfather uses bait, reels in the fish, and cleans it. The grandfather does not bother with explanation, nor does he ask the child to verbalize what he has learned; that will be evident on subsequent trips.

Japanese, Chinese, and Middle Eastern students mimic their childhood instruction in an educational setting. They are usually verbally passive in class, may respond only to direct questions, and learn by observation and practice. Memorization is common. In contrast, American students are assertive, verbal, and learn easily by class discussion and question and answer sessions. Independent research and original, creative work are encouraged.

Cultural values help to control individual behavior, especially learning behavior. Educators have classified two types of learning behavior — *field dependence* and *field independence* — each culturally determined. Cultures such as Asian, Middle Eastern, and most developing countries are field dependent; Americans are usually field independent. This dichotomy can cause conflict when someone from one culture attempts education within the other's system.

Children in many foreign cultures grow up in a society which encourages them to be strongly identified with an extended family.

96

Group achievement is considered far more important than individual identity and accomplishment. Students may work harder for the group than for individual rewards; this follows the Asian childrearing practice of using shame and guilt of the family to control behavior. Autonomy is discouraged and subservience to authority encouraged. Thus Vietnamese children are very obedient in the classroom, and the teacher's status may supercede that of the father. These cultural groups have a formality in interpersonal relations, and they may prefer conformity and structured situations with defined goals. Children of these cultures are *field dependent*. In educational settings they respond well to authority, are inhibited in making remarks, learn by modeling and imitation, work best in groups in structured problem solving, and are less able to think independently.

American students are raised in families where the ties are not as strong, where the democratic process may be evident, and where independence is rewarded. As a result, Americans are *field independent* learners who are active participants in the educational process, enjoy competition and individual success, have a mastery of detail, use inductive reasoning, and often prefer to work independently than in groups.

The international student is then at a distinct disadvantage in our educational system, as American institutions encourage individualized instruction, independent projects and thoughts. Some Latin American countries do not even have their students do individual master theses, but encourage them to work in groups of four![11] An Asian student who has an uncritical acceptance of the authority of his teacher and text, does not develop the critical, questioning faculty so important in Western universities. In countries where the teacher is a supreme authority, never to be contradicted or questioned, demerits may be given to the student seeking additional knowledge.[12]

American instructors are accustomed to teaching methods which are congruent with the learning styles of American students. Studies have found that teachers give less attention to the quiet, passive student of different cultures. Rather than verbally attracting a teacher's attention, these students may simply sit and stare at the teacher.[13]

Many international students regard the teacher in high esteem, and will insist on a formal relationship with the professor. If a teacher who is revered acts too casual or friendly, the student's pride may be hurt. This structured relationship may impede the student from seeking advice, or from developing a give and take in counseling, and perhaps reference, situations.

There are other differences in behaviors between American and foreign students. Classroom behavior may vary greatly. An Arab student may be well behaved in class, yet volunteer no original

97

thinking or questions. This corresponds to field dependent learning behavior. However, a Turkish student may talk to his neighbor the entire class, yet may be a stimulating contributor to class discussions.[14] Japanese students may wander into class late, or not at all: in Japanese universities attendance is not mandatory, but is sporadic and lateness an accepted condition.[15] In the Middle East, Africa and Europe there is a supreme emphasis on the final exam. Students from these areas may ignore mid-terms, quizzes, lab manuals, etc., as they expect their grade to be contingent only on the final. The Chinese and Japanese may suffer from excessive test anxiety. While tests in the West are traditional, tests in the Orient are a novelty and may even be interpreted as an unwarranted invasion of privacy.[16] Plagiarism is a concept many foreign students are unaware of, and may unintentionally violate all rules of scholarship on their initial papers, oblivious of penalties. The strong emphasis in the Middle and Near East on friendship as a great virtue makes cheating an occasional problem. A young Turkish scholar will not cover his paper if surrounded by friends; he would rather take a lower grade than turn down a request from a friend.[17]

Many international students are lost in American classrooms. They have difficulty following lectures and discussions, particularly those in the context of American history, government, and social conditions. The values of Anglo-American culture are institutionalized in educational norms, and the student with different cultural values and learning styles may have difficulty adapting and conforming to school expectations.

Knowledge of Libraries

Using a university library is a bewildering experience for most foreign students. The following description of the Peking University Library, one of the largest in Asia, illustrates the differences between libraries in a developing nation as compared to our own. Imagine the difficulty a Chinese student would have coming from this library to one of America's university libraries.

> Although the library houses three million volumes, the second largest collection of books in China (after the Peking National Library near the Forbidden City), there is no central card catalogue. Instead, I learned on a tour of the building, each department has its own individual catalogue scattered among a labyrinth of corridors and small rooms, most without identifying signs.

> The division serves a purpose. A student may borrow books

only in the field in which he or she is majoring. A math student cannot take out books from the English-language section, not even a volume of Shakespeare's plays or Mark Twain's stories; a history major is barred from the philosophy department, though he may need a book on Plato or Confucius.

After you have found the number of the book you want, you take it to the main charge-out counter in a clamorous room crowded with knots of students shouting to get the attention of the few clerks, who are dressed in long beige smocks to protect them from dust. The library stacks themselves are closed except to a few privileged professors and library-science majors, so students are totally dependent on the clerks, like supplicants.

"At least half the time they take your slip, walk into the stacks, go only a few steps, and without even leaving the main aisle check off 'We don't have it,' " a student studying library science related. One problem, she added, is that most clerks are former peasants or factory workers with only a primary-school education.[18]

Most libraries in developing nations are smaller, with outdated books. Public libraries do not exist, and students may be charged a fee to borrow from their college libraries.[19] Book stacks in countries such as Iraq are closed for security reasons: very few Arabic books exist, and the few that do are kept more for preservation than for use.[20] The concept of library service may be unknown; there may be no reference librarians who instruct in the use of the library. Many libraries are staffed by clerks who merely retrieve books on demand, and would never venture to teach. Libraries are often regarded as a place to study, not research, as they are not considered necessary to the educational process. Instead there is a great reliance on the knowledge of the professor, who either hands the students the books they need, often a single text, or uses a reserve book system. In fact, many libraries are nothing more than reading rooms lined with shelves of textbooks in multiple copies.[21]

The concept of independent library research is an unfamiliar one. One Penn State professor interviewed a new graduate student who claimed he had done "research" in his home country. Upon examining the "research," the professor found it to be nothing but a four-page paper synthesized from a few books, lacking references and footnotes. Many foreign masters and doctoral candidates find themselves writing their first paper in their academic career — even a three-page library research paper can throw them into panic.[22]

American students are taught to be sufficient in a library: they must use the card catalog, retrieve their own books, check them out, and carry them back to their rooms. This idea of self-service is an anathema to some foreign students, especially those from countries with a society structure in which lower classes do the bidding of the wealthy. Librarians may be regarded as nothing more than clerks expected to do their bidding. At Penn State, some international students pay other students to do their library research. For example, wealthy Venezuelans will pay less affluent Puerto Rican students to look up citations, copy articles, and retrieve materials. For foreign students, the less time spent in the library, the better. Many students will spend a fortune on photoduplication; one student ordered 40 doctoral dissertations from University Microforms (at a cost of $400) on a peripheral topic of his dissertation. He told his advisor he liked having them in his home; apparently he felt that their presence gave him legitimacy as a scholar.[23] An international student leader told me that if I took a survey of international students, I would discover that they like our Map Section the best of all library departments. I countered that this was because our collection has maps of the students' countries; but I was informed that the foreign students liked the fact that the Map's staff retrieves the maps and hands them out. In fact, our Map Section is the *only* non self-service section of our library system.

Students also encounter difficulty with the card catalog. Many have trouble alphabetizing, especially those not accustomed to the Roman alphabet. Classification schemes such as Dewey Decimal and Library of Congress may be novel, as many students are accustomed to the Universal Decimal System (UDC), Colon, or Bliss. The American classification systems are often inadequate, and less detailed, in subjects such as Asian literature.[24] Most students expect everything on their country to be under the name of the country in the card catalog — logical perhaps, but not what exists.

Special services and technologies in common use in libraries are new and confusing to many foreign students. In many countries, government information is censored. Imagine the Sudanese student's surprise to find current military training manuals on the open shelf. Inter-library loan is also new, and once discovered, may be used heavily by internationals who do not realize its restrictions. At Penn State, we've had students return to their home countries, American interlibrary books in tow, and students who have asked us to obtain government documents from their countries that are unavailable to the public. Microfiche and film is also new, and students may avoid it because they do not know how to use the machinery. Computer searches are very popular and impressive to international students not yet familiar with computerization. This service helps to circumvent the language difficulties encountered when using an index, but it also prevents a student from learning how to use all library resources effectively. One Latin American student requested a computer search on needs assessment in education. Doing the search on such a broad topic netted many citations at a considerable cost. Months later, the student is still walking around with the search results, now useless, under his arm — a status symbol he enjoys showing off.[25]

Students come to our country with certain notions of what a library is, usually viewing it as an unimportant and unneeded facility. When they discover it necessary to their studies, they are overwhelmed by the vast amount of information available and by the means to obtain it.

Recommendations

It is difficult to make concise recommendations for improving the adjustment of international students to America's educational library systems. Sometimes the only similarities among groups of foreign students is that they are all foreign in America's cultural milieu. "There is no 'foreign students,' rather, there are Indians, Iranians, Chinese . . . all with fairly well defined opinions of each other."[26] Each group of students bring with them a unique cultural background.

What we should do is learn to be more sensitive to contrasting learning styles and be adaptive enough to use diverse educational processes when needed. Let's say you are on a reference desk and a student from China hesitantly approaches you and asks, in halting English, how to find a particular book. *Don't* point to the card catalog and explain about the call number, the directory board, and the stacks. He is from a culture which teaches by observation and imitation, so take him to the card catalog, show him how to use it, and then, if possible, take him to the stacks and put the book in his hand. This step-by-step, observational learning experience will probably have more impact on him because of the learning mode of his culture. Remember to start from a zero base, to talk slowly (not loudly), and avoid library terminology if possible. Repeat your directions more than once if necessary. If students grasp a library research methodology, they should be praised. *Never* cast aspersions on his culture, intelligence, or language, as many foreign students are already in a state of stress, coping with a fear of failure.

Every collegiate librarian should be aware of the composition of foreign student intake, and find out which foreign groups are likely to have the most problems with language and academic adjustment.

Awareness of the library needs of the curricula the students study is also important. An engineering student may have few library needs beyond a study location; education students will use the library often, perhaps studying their own country's education system. A common complaint of foreign students is that libraries have a paucity of materials on their countries. If a university is educating a large group of students from India, then its collection should have current materials on India including an Indian newspaper. If materials are to be heavily demanded, such as reserves, it is a good idea to buy multiple copies. International students need materials longer than others; many are prodigious note takers because of instructional modes in their own cultures.

When the foreign students first arrive on campus, a letter of welcome from the library could be inserted into their orientation folders along with the name and phone number of a library contact. Some librarians have made an extra effort to keep up contacts with international students, such as attending coffees in the International Student Lounge or donating duplicate materials to the Lounge.[27]

Orientation guides can be helpful if designed properly. Some directions, such as how to check out books, should be spelled out step by step. Layout maps of the library should be included. Complicated sentence structure should be avoided, especially those involving passive voice or excessive use of negatives. Unnecessary library terminology should be avoided. The guide should be neither too formal or too informal; eliminate attempts at humor as they may disorient the student rather than informing him and creating a pleasant image of the library.[28] Slide/tape programs, used so often in library instruction, are not effective with most foreign students. Listening to English is a problem for these students, and the disembodied voice of a native speaker enhances the problem. If anything, a videotape with the speaker visible is more effective.

Orientation classes and tours can be an efficient method of library user education if they emphasize the practical aspects of library use, include hands-on experience, and are conducted with small groups. If several sequential classes are to be used, a test has been designed to examine foreign students' knowledge of libraries.[29] This can be a starting point for instruction.

International students can be used as tour assistants or tutors. Students can be divided by language group, and an experienced library user from that group can be appointed to help with the tours, interpreting when English comprehension is difficult. Studies of collegiate counseling services have found that foreign students would rather go to fellow countrymen for help over any other service. This "big brother" system of learning can be encouraged, although there is the occasional risk of the blind leading the blind.[30] On most large campuses, there are clubs representing various nationalities, i.e., Arab Student Association, Chinese Graduate Students, etc. Go to them for help; offer them your services.

It is crucial that library staff be oriented to language and learning differences of the target foreign student population. An in-service training program before the academic year starts can be effective in stemming tensions before they start, and professional staff should be involved. One foreign student told me he found younger staff members, such as student assistants, far nicer and accommodating than older ones. Our University employs many people from the surrounding rural area who have had little or no exposure to those of Chinese, Middle Eastern, or African culture. The anxiety caused by contact with these students may make some employees appear rude or uncooperative. The same student, a leader in the international community, told me that some students will steal books or catalog cards to avoid approaching staff they consider unfriendly to them. A discouraging note, to say the least! Anyone on a service desk must be willing to give patient, friendly help as foreign students struggle to use reference books and indexes they never knew existed. One librarian wrote,"If ever the reference librarian needed to be a teacher and a judge of student's capabilities, it is at this point."[31]

Conclusion

An international student faces many problems in America, including language incompetence, differing cultural values and cues, and misunderstood learning styles. We, the Americans, are often more ignorant of their culture than they of ours. We must learn to look at foreign students as a student first, a foreigner second. "The educators need to be educated," stated Richard Berendzen, "before we can teach foreign students, there is a great deal that we need to learn."[32] Knowledge of a student's background has turned strange and offensive behavior into logical, understandable actions.

While international students need us, we also need to learn from them. Communication is most effective when it results from a symbiotic or synergetic relationship. This is when both parties learn from each other.[33] Our attitudes, behaviors, and instructional practices will do much to minimize the cultural conflicts that do occur and promote an enhanced understanding between librarian-educator and student. Senator William Fulbright, who began the program of international exchange under which 80,000 scholars from 100 countries have studied in the United States, once said:

> Education is a slow moving but powerful force. It may not be fast enough or strong enough to save us from catastrophe, but it is the strongest force available.[34]

103

Notes

1. Malcolm G. Scully, "One Million Foreign Students at U.S. Colleges Seen Likely by 1990," *Chronicle of Higher Education*, 21 October 1981, p1.

2. James Bartoo, Dean of the Graduate School, Pennsylvania State University, February 11, 1982.

3. Carolyn S. Perkins, et al. "A Comparison of the Adjustment Problems of Three International Student Groups," *Journal of College Student Personnel* 18 (September, 1977): 384.

4. Merton Kahne, "Cultural Differences: Whose Troubles Are We Talking About?" *International Educational and Cultural Exchange* 11 (Spring 1976): 38.

5. Leon Carnovsky, "The Foreign Student in the American Library School," *Library Quarterly* 43 (April, 1973): 112.

6. Frank W. Hull, IV, *Foreign Students in the United States of America: Coping Behavior Within the Education Environment* (New York: Praeger, 1978), p35.

7. Mary Genevieve Lewis, "Library Orientation for Asian College Students," *College and Research Libraries* 30 (May, 1969): 267.

8. Montez Bryson, "Libraries Lend Friendship," *International Educational and Cultural Exchange* 10 (February, 1974): 30.

9. John N. Cable, "Foreign Students in the United States," *Improving College and University Teaching* 22 (Winter, 1974): 40.

10. 414 U.S. 563 (1974).

11. Interview with Dr. Joseph Prewitt-Diaz, Association Professor of Bilingual Education, Pennsylvania State University, April 30, 1982.

12. J.R. Penn and M.J. Durham, "Dimensions of Cross-Cultural Interactions," *Journal of College Student Personnel* 19 (May, 1978): 244.

13. George M. Guilmet, "Instructor Reaction to Verbal and Non-Verbal Visual Styles," *Anthropology and Education Quarterly*

10 (Winter, 1979): 251.

14. Kahne, p245.

15. Janice C. Hepworth, "Some Pre-Empirical Considerations for Cross Cultural Attitude Measurements and Persuasive Communications," in *Intercultural and International Communication* (Washington, DC: University Press, 1978), p16.

16. Ibid., p61.

17. Kahne, p245.

18. Fox Butterfield, "How the Chinese Police Themselves," *New York Times Magazine*, 18 April 1982, p52.

19. Lewis, p267.

20. Interview with Wail S. Al-Tikrity, President of International Student Council, Pennsylvania State University, April 20, 1982.

21. Robert Pearce, "The Overseas Student and Library Use — A Special Case for Treatment," in *Proceedings of the Second International Conference on Library User Education*, Oxford University, July 7–10, 1981, ed. Peter Fox (Loughborough, England, 1981), p46.

22. Wail S. Al-Tikrity, April 20, 1982.

23. Ibid.

24. Leon Carnovsky, "The Foreign Student in the American Library School," *Library Quarterly* 43 (April, 1973): 111.

25. Dr. Joseph Prewi6t-Diaz, April 30, 1982.

26. D.C. Johnson, "Ourselves and Others: Comparative Stereotypes," *International Educational and Cultural Exchange* (1974): 24.

27. Lewis, p29–30.

28. Pearce, p48–49.

29. Lewis, p269. The Test is the *American Library Information Test for Foreign Students* (Honolulu: University of Hawaii, 1965). It

gives questions on the card catalog, reference materials, and periodicals without using a timed limit.

30. Paul Pederson, "Personal Problem Solving Resources Used by University of Minnesota Foreign Students," in *Topics in Culture Learning*, ed. Richard W. Brislin (Honolulu: University of Hawaii East-West Center, 1975), vol. 3, p56. ED120273.

31. Lewis, p271.

32. Scully, p1.

33. Lee Thayer, *Communication and Communication Systems* (Homewood, IL: Richard D. Irwin, 1968), p82.

34. William Fulbright, quoted in Brademas, John, "The Importance of Learning About the Rest of the World," *Chronicle of Higher Education* 21 (April 1982): 48.

Bibliography

Adams, Elaine P. "Internationalizing the Learning Resources Center." *College Board Review* 119 (March 1981): 19, 27--28.

Al-Tikrity, Wail S., President of International Student Council, Pennsylvania State University. Interview, 20 April 1982.

Bryson, Montez. "Libraries Lend Friendship." *International Educational and Cultural Exchange* 10 (February 1974): 29--30.

Butterfield, Fox. "How the Chinese Police Themselves." *New York Time Magazine*, April 18, 1982, p32+.

Cable, John N. "Foreign Students in the United States." *Improving College and University Teaching* 22 (Winter 1974): 40--41.

Carnovsky, Leon. "The Foreign Student in the American Library School." *Library Quarterly* 43 (April 1973): 102--25; (July 1973): 199–214.

Daniel, Norman. *The Cultural Barrier; Problems in the Exchange of Ideas*. Edinburgh: University Press, 1975.

Garza, Raymond T. "Affective and Associative Qualities in the Learning Styles of Chicanos and Anglos." *Psychology in the*

Schools 15 (January 1978): 111–15.

Gay, Geneva. "Viewing the Pluralistic Classroom as a Cultural Microcosm." *Educational Research Quarterly* 2 (Winter 1978): 45–55.

Guilmet, George M. "Instructor Reactions to Verbal and Non-Verbal Visual Styles." *Anthropology and Education Quarterly* 10 (Winter 1979): 254–266.

Hagey, A.R. and Joan Hagey. "Meeting the Needs of Students from Other Cultures." *Improving College and University Teaching* 22 (Winter 1974): 42–44.

Harvey, T. Edward, et al. *An Investigation of Cross Cultural Styles Among Traditional and Assimilated Communities of Polynesians and Asian Americans: A Pilot Study*. Paper presented at Annual Conference of the National Association for Asian and Pacific American Education, Honolulu, April 23, 1981. ED 206 785.

Hepworth, Janice C. "Some Pre-Empirical Considerations for Cross-Cultural Attitude Measurement and Persuasive Communications." in *Intercultural and International Education*, ed. by Fred L. Casmir. Washington, DC: University Press of America, 1978.

Huang, Ken. "Campus Mental Health, the Foreigner at Your Desk." *Journal of the American College Health Association* 25 (February 1977): 216–19.

Hull, Frank W., IV. *Foreign Students in the United States of America; Coping Behavior Within the Education Environment*. New York: Praeger, 1978.

Johnson, D.C. "Ourselves and Others: Comparative Stereotypes." *International Educational and Cultural Exchange* 9 (Winter 1974): 24–28.

Joyce, Shana'a. "The Foreign Students: Better Understanding for Better Teaching." *Improving College and University Teaching* 26 (Fall 1978): 243–46.

Kahne, Merton J. "Cultural Differences: Whose Troubles Are We Talking About?" *International Educational and Cultural Exchange* 11 (Spring 1976): 36–40.

Kitand, Margie K. "Early Education for Asian American Children."

Young Children 35 (January 1980): 13–26.

Laosa, Luis M. "Multicultural Education — How Psychology Can Contribute." *Journal of Teacher Education* 28 (May–June 1977): 266–30.

Lewis, Mary Genevieve. "Library Orientation for Asian College Students." *College and Research Libraries* 30 (May 1969): 267–72.

Lynch, James, Assistant Director, International Students' Center, Pennsylvania State University. Interview, 20 April 1982.

Noesjirwan, J. "Attitudes Toward Learning of the Asian Student Studying in the West." *Journal of Cross Cultural Psychology* 1 (December 1970): 393–97.

Opara-Nadi, Bernadette Ego. "The Relationship of Authoritarianism and Dogmatism to Cognitive Style Among American and Third World Students." Doctoral Dissertation, Loyola University of Chicago, 1980.

Parker, Orin D. and Educational Services Staff, American Friends of the Middle East. "Cultural Cues to the Middle Eastern Student." *International Educational and Cultural Exchange* 12 (Fall 1976): 12–18.

Pearce, Robert. "The Overseas Student and Library Use — A Special Case for Treatment." in *Proceedings of the Second International Conference on Library User Education*, Keble College, Oxford, July 7–10, 1981, ed. Peter Fox (Loughborough), 1981.

Pederson, Paul. "Personal Problem Solving Resources Used by University of Minnesota Foreign Students." in *Topics in Culture Learning*, vol. 3, ed. Richard W. Rislin. Honolulu: East-West Center, University of Hawaii, 1975.

Penn, J.R. and Durham, M.J. "Dimensions of Cross Cultural Interactions." *Journal of College Student Personnel* 19 (May 1978): 264–7.

Perkins, Carolyn S., et al. "A Comparison of the Adjustment Problems of Three International Student Groups." *Journal of College Student Personnel* 18 (September 1977): 382–388.

Prewitt-Diaz, Joseph, Associate Professor of Bilingual Education, Pennsylvania State University. Interview, 30 April 1982.

Scully, Malcolm G. "One Million Foreign Students at U.S. Colleges Seen Likely by 1990." *Chronicle of Higher Education* 23 (October 21, 1981): 1+.

Thayer, Lee. *Communication and Communication Systems*. Homewood, IL: Richard D. Irwin, 1968.

Wyatt, Jane Deborah. "Native Involvement in Curriculum Development: The Native Teacher as Cultural Broker." *Interchange: A Journal of Educational Studies* 9 (1978–79): 17–28.

LIBRARY SKILLS
FOR INTERNATIONAL STUDENTS:
FROM THEORY TO PRACTICE

Barbara Brock
University of Toledo

I think I may be the only person here today, perhaps the only person in this country, who has the twin luxury of developing and teaching a university credit course in basic library and information skills designed exclusively for international students. It may strike some of you as ironic that I am teaching a four-hour credit course just to international students, when it can be strongly argued that native speakers also need information search and retrieval skills as well. Nevertheless, what I am going to say in these few minutes can be applied to most introductory library-user education programs.

Briefly, Library Search Strategies is a four-hour credit course offered at the University of Toledo through the College of Education, the American Language Institute, and Carlson Library. Library Search Strategies has been taught since January 1981 to more than 150 students. It is divided into four general areas that acquaint international students with: 1) the public-service role of the library in a democratic society; 2) materials formats, such as books, periodicals, newspapers, print on microform, non-print media, and government publications; 3) the library's physical layout, facilities, and services, available for use; 4) library search strategies based on students' specific information needs. In addition, the international students will be increasing their command of library and search-related vocabulary specific to their fields of study. The course is aimed primarily at students who plan careers in business, science, and engineering.

The design of this course rests on the assumption that students must enter the information process on two simultaneous levels: the functional and the notional.

By the functional level, I mean gaining the language skills to function in an information environment; and gaining the practical skills necessary to use information-access tools. On the functional level, the following problems present themselves:

111

1) Students are unfamiliar with the information vocabulary used in the modern library and in other information centers. Confronted with words like "card catalog," "index," "bibliography," and "audio-visual materials," — I'm sure you can all think of other examples — the average international student, as well as many native speakers, feels he has entered some sort of mysterious netherworld.

2) This feeling of unease increases when the students realize that not only must they learn new vocabulary, but they must also learn a new and highly controlled grammar, "the grammar of subject headings and index language." This grammar often seems arbitrary and seems to violate syntactical forms the students have already learned in English class.

We can realize some of the difficulties international students have with this process by thinking back to the experience all of us have had in looking up phone numbers in the yellow pages. Like all indexes, the phone book uses a specialized controlled language to describe its subject matter. If you want to look up "cars" in the yellow pages, you must look it up using the controlled language of the indexer: "automobiles." You must go from your national language term, "cars," to a controlled language term, "automobiles."

Now imagine going through this process as a non-native speaker. First the student selects, in his native language — Arabic, Spanish, Chinese — the *natural* language term for what he wants: "cars." Now he translates this natural language term into the target language — in this case, English. Then he determines the controlled language equivalent for "cars," that is, "automobiles," in the target language. Then he translates this controlled language term back into his native language. The end of the whole process is that the student understands both in his native language and in the target language the relationship between the controlled and natural terms he has used.

Another example of the peculiarities of the grammar of subject heading language is illustrated by the natural language phrase, "Italian dictionaries of chemistry." To find the heading for this in the *Library of Congress Subject Headings List*, the student must proceed in a hierarchical, or subdivision order to Chemistry — Dictionaries — Italian. Now look what's happened to the syntactical order of the natural language phrase.

Two other problems confront the student regarding subject headings. First he must be made aware of the flexibility of language and vocabulary to describe a subject. What one indexer may call *body language* another will label *non-verbal communication*. There's more than one way to define reality. Second, subject headings

112

reflect social and historical conditions and changes. The term *Negro*, for example, is no longer used, but *Afro-American* is the accepted term. These are fairly simple examples of search and language problems that become more complicated as the students become more sophisticated information researchers.

3) Still on the functional level, in addition to learning the methods of information storage and its linguistic and conceptual classification, students must learn the tools devised to access this information — card catalogs, periodical indexes, abstracts, directories, almanacs, and so forth. Students in business and scientific fields work with very complex information tools — such as *Science Citation Index, Engineering Index*, business ratios, *Moody's Industrial Manuals*, and others. The use of these tools requires an accurate command of the terminology of these fields — again, something in which native and non-native speakers need special instruction.

4) Finally, on the functional level, international students, as well as many native speakers, are unfamiliar with basic search procedures for finding information. Modern researchers begin not only from the premise that information in their field exists; further, they know that there are a series of efficient steps to be taken in a definite order to find this information. It is this series of steps that constitute information search strategies.

These, in brief, are functional problems that international students have in gaining the language skills to function in an information environment and the practical skills needed to use information access tools.

But in addition to providing necessary skills to overcome these functional problems, teachers must also address students' needs on an attitudinal level. This level I call the notional level. International students must overcome a natural distrust of information institutions like libraries, and must prepare themselves to enter a different cultural setting for information. Key problems on this notional level include the following:

1) Students need to be made aware of the process by which an information need is identified. Only then can they begin to sort out the essential first step: separating "what I know" from "what I need to know."

113

2) International students are unacquainted with the variety of information available to researchers in various fields. Many students, for example, are surprised to find that the U.S. government is a major producer of information in scientific and business fields. In my course, Library Search Strategies, I spend several sessions in this area alone.

3) Students are ignorant of the variety of ways to access this information. Fundamentally, they regard information as a collection of random facts, rather than looking for an information network that they can tap into and retrieve information about their professional fields.

4) Students are unfamiliar with the process by which information can be synthesized into knowledge. They need to know the bases on which information can be evaluated, the relevant information sorted from the inappropriate, and that a conclusion can be drawn from this information and supported in a clear, concise manner. For example, the final assignment in Library Search Strategies is for the students not only to choose a research topic and prepare a twenty-item bibliography, but the topic must be stated as a thesis statement. In other words, requiring the students to choose and support a point of view, for example the thesis statement: *Capital punishment prevents crime*, helps them to begin the process of gathering, evaluating, and using information in a meaningful way.

These four points then are the notional problems international students, as well as many native speakers, encounter when working with information: identifying information needs; gaining familiarity with the variety of information available; gaining familiarity with the variety of ways to access this information; and synthesizing information into knowledge. I want to emphasize again that not all of these points are unique to international students, but are common to all students at both the high school and college levels.

While students' information needs can be separated into these two categories, the functional and the notional, they cannot be treated separately. Students cannot acquire the necessary skills to retrieve and use information efficiently unless they can overcome their mistrust of the library. And, on the other side, they cannot feel at ease in an information setting without knowing some of the skills necessary to use that setting properly. The point here is that *both* sets of problems must be addressed simultaneously.

In 1980, the American Language Institute, an intensive English language institute that prepares students to enter a university, along with Carlson Library and the College of Education, agreed to fund a four-hour credit course in library search strategies for international students. The University of Toledo has an international student population of about 1,200, and it continues to grow. Many of the students are from Middle Eastern countries, and a smaller number come from Latin America and Africa. There are almost no European students in the university.

With this group as the target population, I developed a ten-week course, Library Search Strategies 310:101. The first half of the course outlines the major information formats used in the Carlson Library — books, periodicals, newspapers, annual reports, pamphlets, microform, non-print media, and maps. In each section students are taught the vocabulary of each format. They need to have a good command of this basic vocabulary — author, title, publisher, copyright, volume, issue, bound, unbound, and so forth, before they begin to use access tools like the card catalog and periodical indexes. Without a functional vocabulary, it would be very difficult to teach them how to interpret the information found in these tools. In the second half of the course, students are prepared to learn the skills necessary to search for information in the library. Within a structured search-strategy approach, they are required to prepare a twenty-item bibliography of books, periodical and newspaper articles, and government documents, defending a thesis topic of their choice. This assignment also serves to pull together the students' functional and notional grasp of information skills and to enable them to enter the library in a concrete search for information.

Now, in developing this course, two problems leap out at us: 1) the course has limited application outside the particular situation at Carlson Library, because most institutions do not have the money, time, or resources to develop and sustain such a course. 2) The students' information skills are not immediately connected to other areas of their education. I strongly feel that information skills, if the students are to be able to transfer them outside the classroom, ought to be course-related — that is, students must use them to complete actual research assignments, not just the ones devised for Library Search Strategies in order to test these skills.

As a result, I am constantly looking for ways to apply some of the experience accumulated in the ten-week course to a wider setting — reaching more students for a shorter time. At present, I have two outreach programs: one official, and the other just getting underway. The first program is already established with the ALI. It consists of a two-session library-user education component integrated with the ALI reading curriculum. I am able to offer basic orientation and instruction through lectures and self-guided walking tours developed at Carlson Library. This program reaches about 150 students every quarter. During the first 50-minute lecture session in the library, students are introduced to some of the specialized vocabulary of library and research formats — books, serials, the author/title catalog, the subject card catalog, indexes, and encyclopedias. During the second session, the students working in small groups, complete self-guided walking tours of Carlson Library. By asking students to answer selected questions at various reference stops along the way, these tours combine both orientation to the physical layout of the library with basic instruction. The walking tour asks them to find an author in the card catalog, see if the library carries a certain periodical, find an entry in the *Readers' Guide to Periodical Literature*, locate a current periodical and a back issue of the same periodical and bring them both back to class. They return to the classroom and have the opportunity to discuss their experiences.

No formal method has yet been arrived at for evaluating the success of these sessions. However, it is a great pleasure to find an international student who has previously taken my course helping an American student with the *Readers' Guide.*

In addition to working with the ALI faculty and students, my second outreach attempt is to establish contact and cooperate with regular university faculty who find that they have a large number of international students in their courses who are unable to do basic research necessary to complete class assignments. The students don't know such basic things as how to use the card catalog, read a call number, or what a periodical index is. The professors do not have time to give library-user instruction to these students. In one course in the History of the Middle East, I work with the professor to give his international students special library-user instruction.

Developing this type of course-related library-user instruction is one of the most effective ways of ensuring the transfer of library skills to meet immediate information needs.

To conclude: international students present special problems in gaining access to the vast network of information in academic libraries and in the professional world. They have problems in functioning in an information environment, in understanding the specialized vocabulary of library research and subject heading language found in access tools, and even problems with simple word-by-word or letter-by-letter alphabetization to understanding some of the fundamental filing rules of the Library of Congress subject card catalog. They need to learn how to read call numbers, as well as how to interpret complex information in an entry from a catalog card or a periodical index. And finally, and probably the most crucial of all, they need to be able to pull together and synthesize seemingly random points of information data into a coherent pattern of understanding — in other words, to be able to gather, evaluate, and use information effectively.

DIAGRAM 1.

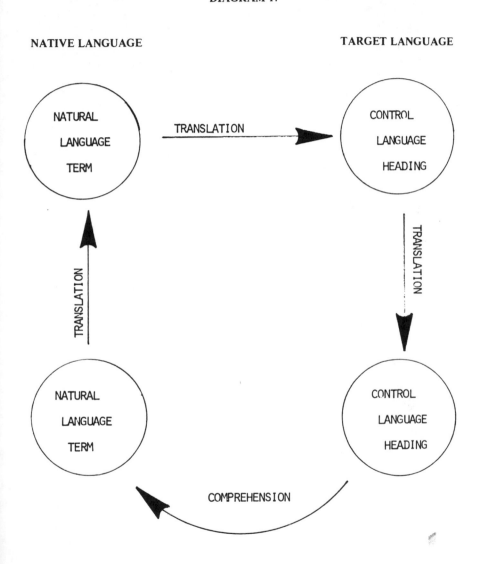

NATIVE LANGUAGE

TARGET LANGUAGE

NATURAL LANGUAGE TERM

TRANSLATION

CONTROL LANGUAGE HEADING

TRANSLATION

TRANSLATION

NATURAL LANGUAGE TERM

CONTROL LANGUAGE HEADING

COMPREHENSION

THE TEACHING OF
INFORMATION FOR KNOWLEDGE:
A PROCESS MODEL
FOR BIBLIOGRAPHIC INSTRUCTION

Gloria R. Freimer
Angelo Wallace
University of Toledo

Introduction

The idea of an information explosion conjures up the notion of a big "bang." Rather, the universe of information can be characterized today as one constantly expanding. The characteristics of this information universe are complex interrelated disciplinary structures, each of which has its own order and is related to other structures in an orderly way. Citation indexes are graphic illustrations of these structures and the relationships imbedded in them.

In addition, information has become a specialized branch of knowledge and is characterized by its own hermetic or "closed" structure. The elements which make up this structure are the organization, storage and dissemination of knowledge according to specified rules or codes, as exemplified by libraries. These structures must be dealt with in both interactive and integrative ways in order to be understood and successfully used. Since this structure of information is closed, scholars and would-be scholars need a key to open it. Bibliographic instruction provides this key.

In order to arrive at an orderly and logical planning of instructional activities in our field, it is necessary to develop a theory of instruction based on a theory of human learning. This in turn must be founded on a theory of knowledge. It is also essential that this theory of knowledge be based on a paradigm or "world view" of the informational/instructional activities of society and human beings. Our "world view" derives from the process philosophies of John Dewey and Alfred North Whitehead who state that education is process, and that knowledge is not a product. Our theories of learning and instruction derive from this paradigm, as does the model presented here. A way of comprehending that complex of societal and human activities is through the formation and application of theory. Theory formation is the tool that allows us to impose a testable structure on the reality of the world. Some observations on

119

theory are required before presenting some features of our learning model.

Necessity for Models of Learning Theory

All human activities share a number of similar characteristics: a body of knowledge or information to be mastered or transferred; a social or organizational environment where the activity takes place; the role demanded of the individual (passive, reactive, etc.); the element of time; a set of objectives (either defined by the individual or the organization) which are based on a larger goal, i.e., information sophistication in our case.

In order to integrate the above characteristics into an operational whole, planning is required for the necessary testing of the proposed activities. This planning can be facilitated by the application of theory. Theory, as defined by Fiegl, is a set of assumptions from which can be derived, by scientific procedures, a larger set of empirical laws, which allow us to begin to impose a "structure" or "plan" upon our proposed activities.

The Nature and Value of Theory

Theory is not impractical, it is not speculation, it is not supposition, it is not the ideal, it is not a set of values, nor, finally, is it a set of operational "oughts." Theory is a definition (as exemplified by Fiegl's earlier definition), and it is for our purposes, as agreement on terminology about facts, concepts, presumptions, and assumptions about the learner and the learning environment.

What value can one derive from theory formation? The value of theory can be identified at two levels: at the lowest level it provides us with "sensitizing concepts" which serve the purpose of identifying certain specific aspects of the bibliographic instruction activity. At the middle level it provides us with the "integrating concepts" which serve to relate lower level concepts into concepts of great observation and analytical power.

Let us now quickly review the models of learning theory currently existing in our secondary and higher educational systems. The preponderant model is one that is based on the notion of a body of knowledge that must be learned. This body of knowledge is transferred to the student who then is required to master it. This is the oldest model, generally known as the Essentialist or Realist model. More recent models such as Piaget's and Skinner deal with the acquisition of knowledge as part of the psychological development and needs satisfaction of the individual. The introduction of computers into teaching/learning environment has also given rise to a Cybernetic model of instructional theory. Such a model views learning as a "mechanically" interactive activity in a logically organized sequence, providing immediate feedback to the learner. The models of instruction based on these learning theories are aimed primarily at young learners, where a developmental theory of learning is appropriate. In Bibliographic Instruction at the college level we are generally dealing with adult learners, learners who have by now developed a basic comprehension of their role in a learning situation. In addition, they are quite ready to explore and modify that role in an instructional/informational environment.

In addition, the above models do not take into consideration social and institutional components. In any instructional setting, learning is not a purely internal activity, but takes place within a social/institutional context generally characterized by a definite structure and complex organizing concept.

A Definition of Bibliographic Instruction

We in Bibliographic Instruction seem to pay lip service to the complexity of information and the need for training. However, the model existing today is generally the traditional Essentialist teacher/student one. Our Bibliographic Instruction Program uses a model which takes into account the needs of the organization and of the individual and which recognizes the interactive and integrative nature of that process at the theoretical and operational level. Our aims are not primarily the development of library-use skills, but rather the facilitation of the whole process of learning. After all, learning to use the library is really about "learning to learn." Our model takes into consideration both the individual's needs for information/knowledge and the reality of the complexity of the informational setting (the library). We define Bibliographic Instruction as the activity that facilitates the process of interaction between the individual and the complex organization (the library). When it is successful, that interaction is characterized by a continuous wave motion between the two dimensions resulting in the acquisition of skills and information. Learning is defined within the model as a process (the wave motion) or the ability of the individual to satisfy his own needs by functioning efficiently in the organizational setting and being able to use its resources for his own purposes.

Implications of the Model

What are some of the implications of the model for Bibliographic Instruction activity?

BIBLIOGRAPHIC INSTRUCTION
AS VIEWED INTERACTIVELY AND INTEGRATIVELY**

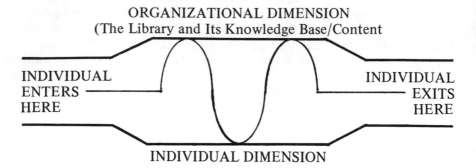

ORGANIZATIONAL DIMENSION
(The Library and Its Knowledge Base/Content

INDIVIDUAL   INDIVIDUAL
ENTERS   EXITS
HERE   HERE

INDIVIDUAL DIMENSION

** Model allows for resolution of the conflict (learning) existing between the organizational and individual dimensions. Based on Getzels-Guba.

1. It clarifies the complex relationship between the individual and the organizational dimensions;

2. it is independent of particular formats of information and/or tools;

3. it prepares the student to be an independent learner and to be an expert in the use of information; and

4. it allows for constant revision of program objectives to fit the changing nature of the environment.

Some Conclusions about the Model

Some conclusions that can be drawn from the application of theory/model formation upon bibliographic instruction activities are:

1. It allows a discussion "paradigm" or "world view" to emerge;

2. we expect the model to inform all our planning;

3. it allows experimental applications of teaching tools and

122

techniques (self-guided walking tour, course integration, development of special instructional activities); and

4. provides the theoretical pedagogical structure upon which to design and implement cohesive bibliographic instruction activities on our campus.

Bibliography

Rao Aluri, "Application of Learning Theories to Library-Use Instruction," *Libri* (September 1981): 140–152.

Henry P. Cole, *Process Education: The New Direction in Elementary-Secondary Schools* (Englewood Cliffs, NJ: Educational Technology Publications, 1972).

Daniel E. Griffiths, *Administrative Theory* (New York: Appleton-Century-Crofts, 1959).

Thomas S. Kuhn, *The Structure of Scientific Revolutions* (Chicago: University of Chicago Press, 1970).

BIBLIOGRAPHIC INSTRUCTION
AND THE LEARNING PROCESS:

SELECTED BACKGROUND READING

Aluri, Rao. "Application of Learning Theories to Library-Use Instruction." *Libri* 31 (2); August 1981, 140–152.

Aluri, Rao and Mary Reichel. *Evaluation of Student Learning in Library-Use Instructional Programs Based on Cognitive Learning Theory*. Paper presented July 1981 at Oxford, England: Second International Conference on User Education.

Ausubel, David P. *Educational Psychology: A Cognitive View*. New York: Holt, Rinehart & Winston, 1968.

Ausubel, David P. and Floyd G. Robinson. *School Learning: An Introduction to Educational Psychology*. New York: Holt, Rinehart & Winston, 1969.

Blue, Terry W. *The Teaching and Learning Process*. Washington, DC: National Education Association, 1981. (Analysis & Action Series.)

Davis, R.H., L.T. Alexander and S.L. Yelon. *Learning Systems Design: An Approach to the Improvement of Instruction*. New York: McGraw-Hill, 1974.

Diamond, R.R., et al. *Instructional Development for Individualized Learning in Higher Education*. Englewood Cliffs, NJ: Educational Technology Publications, 1975.

Ellison, John W. "Effective Library Instruction and the Learning Process." *Catholic Library World* 53 (4); November 1981, 182–184.

Fuller, Robert G., ed. *Multidisciplinary Piagetian-Based Programs for College Freshmen*. 3d ed. Lincoln, NE: Adapt, University of Nebraska, 1978.

Gerlach, V.S. and D.P. Ely. *Teaching and Media: A Systematic Approach*. Englewood Cliffs, NJ: Prentice-Hall, 1971.

Hullfish, H. Gordon and Philip G. Smith. *Reflective Thinking: The Method of Education*. New York: Dodd, Mead & Co., 1961.

Kobelski, Pamela and Mary Reichel. "Conceptual Frameworks for Bibliographic Instruction." *Journal of Academic Librarianship* 7 (2); May 1981, 73–77.

Kubinec, William, et al. "Freshman Abstract Reasoning Project," in *Proceedings for a National Conference on Teaching Decision-Making: Guided Design*, 1980. May 28, 29, 30. Morgantown, WV: West Virginia University, 1980.

Lawson, A. and J.W. Renner. "Teaching for Thinking: A Piagetian Perspective." *Today's Education* 65; 1976, 38--41.

Mellon Constance A. and Edmund Sass. "Perry and Piaget: Theoretical Framework for Effective College Course Development," *Educational Technology* 21 (5); May 1981, 29–33.

Merrill, M.D. and R.D. Tennyson. *Teaching Concepts: An Instructional Design Guide*. Englewood Cliffs, NJ: Educational Technology Publication, 1977.

Oberman-Soroka, Cerise. *Petals Around a Rose: Abstract Reasoning and Bibliographic Instruction*. Chicago, IL: ALA, 1980. n.p.

Oberman-Soroka, Cerise and Katina Strauch, eds. *Theories of Bibliographic Education: Designs for Teaching*. New York: Bowker, 1982.

Tickton, Sidney, ed. *To Improve Learning*. New York: Bowker, 1970, vol. 1.

Tomlinson-Keasey, Carol and Debra C. Eisert. "Can Doing Promote Thinking in the College Classroom?" *Journal of College Student Personnel* 19; March 1978, 99–105.

Treffinger, Donald J. and Jaclyn R. Huber. "Designing Instruction in Creative Problem-Solving: Preliminary Objectives & Learning Hierarchies." *Journal of Creative Behavior* 9; Fourth Quarter, 260–266.

Wales, Charles E. and Robert A. Stager. *Guided Design*. Morgantown, WV: West Virginia University, 1977.

Wildman, Terry M. "Cognitive Theory and the Design of Instruction." *Educational Technology* 21 (7); July 1981, 14--20.

Wildman, Terry M. and John K. Burton. "Integrating Learning Theory with Instructional Design." *Journal of Instructional Development* 4 (3); September 1981.

LIBRARY ORIENTATION AND INSTRUCTION – 1981

Hannelore B. Rader

The following annotated bibliography of materials on orienting users to libraries and on instructing them in the use of reference and other resources covers publications from 1981. A few items from 1980 have been included because information about them was not available in time for the 1980 listing. A few items have not been annotated because the compiler was unable to secure a copy of these items.

Included are publications on user instruction in all types of libraries and for all types of users from young children to adults. The list has been divided into categories by type of library.

Items in foreign languages, though numerous, have been excluded.

1981 publications indicate an increase over 1980 publications of 27 percent. Except for school libraries all categories show an increase in number of publications compared to 1980 as follows:

academic libraries	33%
public libraries	67%
school libraries	–22%
special libraries	25%
all levels	32%

Though most of the items were published in the library literature, a few items appear in non-library publications. In 1981 there are also an increased number of books published about user instruction. Concern with evaluation and theoretical framework of user instruction is also apparent from the listed publications, However, the majority number of the items listed are still program descriptions.

COMMUNITY COLLEGE LIBRARIES

Baker, Robert K. *Doing Library Research: An Introduction for Community College Students.* Boulder, CO: Westview Press, 1981.

Taylor, Lee R., Jr. "Teaching Freshman Research Methods." *Teaching English in the Two-Year College* 7 (Fall, 1980): 37–40.

COLLEGE AND UNIVERSITY LIBRARIES

Adalian, Paul T. and Ilene F. Rockman. *BLISS: Basic Library Information Sources and Strategies: A Handbook for Library 101.* ERIC Document Reproduction Service, 1981. ED 200 202.
   This is a manual to acquaint college students with the California Polytechnic Library and search strategies. Included are glossaries of library terms, symbols and abbreviations.

Adams, Mignon. "Comment on Bibliographic Instruction in Academic Libraries." *Catholic Library World* 53 (April, 1981): 397–399.
   Discusses the lack of adequate media materials for academic library instruction available commercially. Several other librarians provide additional comments on this topic and concur that commercial library media companies ought to produce such materials.

Aluri, Rao. "Application of Learning Theories to Library Use Instruction." *Libri* 31 (August, 1981): 140–152.
   This paper discusses library use instruction programs through the perspective of various learning theories. The author explains the cognitive structure perspective, the conditioning perspective and the cybernetic perspective and applies them to library use instruction.

Anstine, Francisca A. "Library Instruction and Disabled Individuals." *Illinois Libraries* 63 (September, 1981): 535–539.
   Author discusses importance of providing disabled library users with library skills. Efforts in this regard at the Health Sciences Library, University of Illinois, Urbana are described. Library instruction programs for the disabled need to take into consideration the various handicaps, such as visual, mobile and hearing.

Anwar, Mumtaz A. "Education of the User of Information." *International Library Review* 13 (October, 1981): 365–383.

Author provides an overview of the status of user education on an international basis, summarizes resources for user education and programs, and talks about the lack of available training programs for Pakistani scholars. Also reported is a survey of Pakistani scholars to assess their library instruction experiences. A national user education program is outlined.

Ballam, Susan H. "Developing a Bibliographic Instruction Unit for the College Library." *Catholic Library World* 53 (November, 1981): 180–181.

Author outlines specific steps to follow to create a comprehensive library instruction program in a college library, using the Rosemont College in Pennsylvania as an example.

Barry, Carol. *An Illinois Union List of Commercially-Produced Audiovisual Materials for Bibliographic Instruction.* ERIC Document Reproduction Service, 1981. ED 203 881.

This union list of library instruction materials produced commercially is based on a survey of 37 academic libraries in Illinois. Included are only materials published after 1965 and on the high school level or above.

Bechtel, Joan. "Collegial Management Breeds Success." *American Libraries* 12 (November, 1981): 605–607.

At Dickinson College in Pennsylvania librarians have been successful in becoming more significant partners with faculty in the educational process by reorganizing the library on a collegial level using participatory management, library-faculty liaisons and library instruction. This reorganization has generated an exciting professional climate.

"Bibliographic Instruction: Think Tank Recommendations for Bibliographic Instruction." *College and Research Library News* 42 (December, 1981): 394–398.

Summarizes the recommendations for bibliographic instruction developed by a Think Tank of first generation bibliographic instruction librarians who met at the ACRL Bibliographic Instruction Pre-Conference in San Francisco in June 1981. The recommendations address the integration of bibliographic instruction with schools of library science. The importance of research and publications relating to bibliographic instruction is stressed.

Biglin, Karen and others. *Your NAU Library Workbook*. ERIC Document Reproduction Service, 1981. ED 194 117.

This illustrated library skills workbook is aimed at university students to introduce them to the collection, research tools and research process.

Binder, Michael B. and others. "Library Instruction by Videotape and Lecture: A Case Study." *Urban Academic Librarian* 1 (Spring, 1981): 16--18.

Describes and evaluates experiences with a library instruction program in videotape format and assignment-oriented library lectures. Faculty prefer the use of the lectures which utilize transparencies and handouts to the videotape which was produced in-house at Fairleigh Dickinson University.

Blackie, Edna and Joan M. Smith. "Student Information Needs and Library User Education." *Education Libraries Bulletin* 24 (1981): 16–23.

Carmichael, James V., Jr. "Hand-Off Instruction: A Study of the Effectiveness of a Media-Based Library Instruction Module." *Georgia Librarian* 18 (November, 1981): 4–8.

Georgia College in Georgia adapted its English 102 library instruction program to slide-tape and video format and evaluated the traditional lecture format as well as the new media formats.

Chapman, Liz. "Report on the Second International Conference on Library User Education." *New Library World* 82 (October, 1981): 186–188.

Author summarizes the Second International Conference on Library User Education in Oxford, July 1981 and provides her own impressions of this remarkable conference.

Chung, Myoung and others. *Report on the Development of Six Point-of-Use Audio-Visual Library Instructional Programs*. ERIC Document Reproduction Service, 1981. ED 202 466.

Describes six point-of-use audiovisual programs developed at Rutgers University library using 16mm filmstrip cartridges. User evaluation data is also reported.

Clark, D. and others. *The Travelling Workshops Experiment in Library User Education*. London: British Library, 1981.

This is another one of the Research and Development Reports published by the British Library and describes a four-year project to promote and demonstrate library use education in academic institutions in Great Britain. The project included workshops, learning materials packages and an assessment by ASLIB. The workshop and materials involved the areas of biology, mechanical engineering, social welfare, British history and health studies. A practical self-instructional approach was utilized. It was found that library instruction is still more dependent on the involvement of the academic staff.

Clement, Russell T. and others. *Using the Joseph F. Smith Library*. ERIC Document Reproduction Service, 1981. ED 201 328.
Describes a two-hour credit course in English at Brigham Young University which includes a library instruction package. The course, which teaches library skills and research writing, features discussions, exercises, search strategies, etc.

Condon, Patrick. *Will the User Sink or Swim? Utilization of User Education Resources to Advantage*. ERIC Document Reproduction Service, 1981. ED 201 327.
Discusses library instruction for students in higher education in Australia. Gives a history, state-of-the-art and description of the Australian database of library instruction materials.

Costa, Joseph J. *A Directory of Library Instruction Programs in Pennsylvania Academic Libraries*. ERIC Document Reproduction Service, 1980. ED 200 225.
The directory summarizes library instruction programs in 102 Pennsylvania academic libraries.

Cottam, Keith M. and Connie V. Dowell. "A Conceptual Planning Method for Developing Bibliographic Instruction Programs." *Journal of Academic Librarianship* 7 (September, 1981): 223–228.
The authors propose and describe a theoretical, instructional development model for bibliographic instruction in academic libraries. Such a model should facilitate the planning process in academic libraries and bring about more efficient and relevant bibliographic instruction programs. Planning tables are included.

DeWit, Linda and others. "Bibliographic Instruction. Library Seminars: Keeping Faculty Informed." *College and Research Library News* 42 (October, 1981): 326–327.
Describes the use of library seminars for faculty at Michigan State University as a vehicle to inform them as well as graduate students about new reference tools and library services.

Fjallbrant, Nancy and others. "Self-Paced Exercises for Library Orientation." *Aslib Proceedings* 33 (1981): 251–253.

The authors point out the need for economical and effective methods of library orientation. The self-paced tour with exercises is recommended.

Foster, Jocelyn H. "Influence Through User Education – A Strategy for Campus Librarians." *Canadian Library Journal* 38 (February, 1981): 35–37.

Author advocates a more active approach to the integration of library instruction into the academic curriculum on the part of librarians. Students must be taught to be critical and analytical through an understanding of the bibliographic structure.

Frank, Virginia and Elaine Trzebiatowski. "Designing Search Strategies: An Approach to Library Instruction." *Illinois Libraries* 63 (October, 1981): 573–575.

Author describes the library instruction program based on the search strategy method at Millikin University in Illinois.

Freedman, Janet, "A Right to Service Academic Libraries and Adult Learners." *Lifelong Learning: The Adult Years* 5 (December, 1981): 10–12.

The article is based on a survey from a British educator of selected American academic institutions as to library services for adult learners. New guidelines are needed and it is hoped that most helpful responses will come from the library instruction movement.

Frick, Elizabeth. *Library Research Guide to History: Illustrated Search Strategy and Sources.* Ann Arbor, MI: Pierian Press, 1980.

This guide provides a search strategy for term papers on historical subjects. It uses a sample search topic to introduce college upper-level undergraduates to reference sources in history.

Gavryck, Jacquelyn and others. *Library Research Curriculum Materials for a One-Credit Course.* ERIC Document Reproduction Service, 1981. ED 203 884.

This manual gives the course outline, objectives, pre-test, exercises and materials for ten sessions for a course taught at the undergraduate level at the State University of New York at Albany library.

Getchell, Charles M. and Robert W. Melton. "Bibliographic Instruction.

A Non-Credit/Non-Graded Course at the University of Kansas."
College and Research Libraries News 42 (June, 1981): 173–174.

Librarians at the University of Kansas at Lawrence have developed a non-credit/non-graded course for basic research skills described here. This seven-week course seems to be a successful venture at a medium-sized university with an enrollment of 23,000 students.

Gilliam, Bodil H. "Beyond Bibliographic Instruction." *Southeastern Librarian* (Spring, 1981): 8–10.

Instruction librarians are advised to not only gain faculty support for their programs but to also obtain the support of other groups within the academic environment. Libraries at the University of West Florida held a workshop for secretaries to build a support group for bibliographic instruction among them. The workshop is described in detail. Technical services, serials, special collections and government documents librarians contributed to the workshop.

Gover, Harvey R. *Keys to Library Research on the Graduate Level: A Guide to Guides.* Washington, DC: University Press of America, Inc., 1981.

The aim of this publication is to be a graduate student's library survival kit. It gives brief descriptions of campus libraries and librarians as information providers. Major emphasis is on explaining the card catalog, the LC system, computer prepared indexes and abstracts and bibliographies. Non-book materials and automated retrieval services are also discussed briefly.

Gwinn, Nancy E. and Warren J. Haas. "Crisis in the College Library." *AGB Reports* (March-April, 1981): 41–45.

This article discusses the budget problems in academic libraries as related to materials purchases, the importance of resource sharing, interlibrary loan, cooperative collection development, collection evaluation and librarians' involvement in the curriculum. A number of innovative library-instruction programs are outlined.

Hardesty, Larry. "The Utilization of Academic Librarians as Academic Librarians." *Academe* (February-March, 1981): 50.

This is a letter replying to M.R. Yerburgh's article on utilizing academic librarians as classroom teachers. Hardesty feels that librarians can make their most significant contributions in the educational process by being partners with faculty through library instruction, orientation and reference.

Harding, Alan G. "The Effectiveness of Library Instruction." *ISG News* 17 (April, 1981): 9–11.

Hodina, Alfred and others. *Information Resources in the Sciences and Engineering. A Laboratory Workbook.* ERIC Document Reproduction Service, 1981. ED 205 178.

This work introduces upper-level undergradute and graduate students to traditional and computerized library resources. Included are exercises, a list of 66 subject guides to the literature of science and technology and a bibliography of 81 references.

Hofmann, Lucinda A. "Educate the Educator: A Possible Solution to an Academic Librarian's Dilemma." *Journal of Academic Librarianship* 7 (July, 1981): 161–163.

This describes a faculty library orientation workshop presented at Miami-Dade Community College South Campus for 15 hours and one hour in-house credit. Objectives, planning, teaching and evaluation of this workshop are described.

Hopkins, Frances L. "User Instruction in the College Library. Origins, Prospects, and a Practical Program." In *College Librarianship*, pp. 173–204, edited by William Miller and D.S. Rockwood. Metuchen, NJ: Scarecrow, 1981.

Discusses development of the library instruction concept with emphasis on the 1980s. Provides rationale for the importance of library instruction as a serious professional specialty and shows its relationship to reference service. Elaborates the possible future of library instruction and gives practical suggestions for establishing teacher-librarians as specialists who are different from traditional public service librarians.

Jackson, Miles M. *Teachers College Libraries in Papua New Guinea.* A Report for the Asia Foundation, the Library Services and the Teacher Education Divisions of the Department of Education, Government of Papua New Guinea. ERIC Document Reproduction Service, 1981. ED 207 600.

Paper discusses current status of libraries in eleven teacher colleges in Papua. Twenty recommendations are offered to improve existing conditions including implementation of full courses in library skills.

Jean, Lorraine H. *Introducing the College-Bound Student to the Academic Library: A Case Study.* ERIC Document Reproduction Service, 1981. ED 200 226.

Describes academic library orientation workshops held at the

University of Vermont to acquaint college-bound high school seniors with resources in academic libraries. Exercises are included.

Jenkins, Kathleen H. *The Library Skills Learning Package: An Evaluation.* ERIC Document Reproduction Service, 1981. ED 195 277.
Evaluates the effectiveness of the Library Skills Learning Package, a printed, self-contained instructional program with exercises used by students of Eastern Illinois University. Evaluations are appended.

Jones, David E. "Bibliographic Instruction for M. Ed. Students." *Education Libraries Bulletin* 24 (1981): 24–39.

Kartis, Alexia M. and Annette J. Watters. "Library Research Strategies for Education Researchers." *Capstone Journal of Education* 2 (Summer, 1981): 22–32.
Gives information sources and retrieval techniques for searching recent educational literature. Specific reference tools are described and types of reference sources are discussed.

Kay, K.L. "Library Orientation." *Journal of Business Education* 57 (October, 1981): 3.
Explains a program of library instruction at Tiffin University using self-explanatory transparency programs.

Kenney, Donald J. "Role of Technical Services Librarians in Library Instruction." *Southeastern Librarian* (Spring, 1981): 11–13.
Describes the involvement of technical services librarians in the bibliographic instruction program at the College of Charleston and discusses the rationale for such involvement on a supportive, cooperative and active level.

Kerka, Sandra and others. "LIP Service: The Undergraduate Library Instruction Program at the Ohio State University." *Journal of Academic Librarianship* 7 (November, 1981): 279–282.
Describes the library instruction program at Ohio State University where an automated library system is in place. The program reaches 8,600 first-year undergraduate students in the fall term and up to 10,000 students in a year. The planning and implementation of this program are described in detail.

Key, Janet and Thomas A. Tollman. *Videotape as an Aid to Bibliographic Instruction.* ERIC Document Reproduction Service,

1981. ED 206 319.

Discusses use of videotaped lectures in the undergraduate library instruction program at the University of Nebraska. Describes the production of specific videotapes and reports results of a survey to compare the videotape method with a slide lecture method.

King, David N. and John C. Ory. "Effects of Library Instruction on Student Research: A Case Study." *College and Research Libraries* 42 (January, 1981): 31–41.

Points out the importance of evaluating library instruction programs. One area that could be evaluated is the behavioral effect of library instruction on the students' use of the library. A comparison of student use of resources, services, libraries and catalogs was developed at the University of Illinois' Undergraduate Library to evaluate the instruction program. Findings indicate significant differences between students who have library instruction and those who did not have any.

Kirk, Thomas. "Library Administrators and Instruction Librarians: Improving Relations." *Journal of Academic Librarianship* 6 (January, 1981): 345.

This editorial advocates closer cooperation and communication between library administrators and instruction librarians to work on improving and strengthening user instruction.

Kirkendall, Carolyn. *Directions for the Decade: Library Instruction in the 1980s.* Ann Arbor, MI: Pierian Press, 1981.

These are the papers presented at the 10th Annual Conference on Library Orientation for Academic Libraries held at Eastern Michigan University, May 8–9, 1980. They include an article by John Lubans on assessing library instruction, Frances Hopkins' Bibliographic Instruction; An Emerging Professional Discipline and an article by Nancy Fjallbrant on evaluating user education. Michael Keresztesi discusses bibliographic instruction in the 1980s and beyond, John Kupersmith describes library signage and Mary Huston-Miyamoto provides information on computer-assisted instruction. Summaries of a panel on politics and personalities in bibliographic instruction featuring Roger Fromm, Bonnie King, Cerise Oberman-Soroka and Virginia Tiefel followed by a panel giving post-prandial reactions by Suzanne A. Aiardo, Donald Kenney, Marilyn Lutzker, Wayne Meyer and Roger Sween are also included. The proceedings conclude with a 1979 review of the literature by Hannelore B. Rader.

Kirkendall, Carolyn. "Library Instruction. A Column of Opinion." *Journal of Academic Librarianship* 7 (May, 1981): 95–96.

In this column Nancy Fjallbrant from Chalmers University of Technology in Sweden, Joan Ormondroyd from Cornell University, Ross La Baugh from Southeastern Massachusetts University and Lois M. Pausch from the University of Illinois address the issue of evaluating library instruction.

Kirkendall, Carolyn. "Library Instruction. A Column of Opinion." *Journal of Academic Librarianship* 7 (July, 1981): 164–165.

This column addresses the effectiveness of library skills programs. Responses to the statement that librarians' professional sense and experience are probably the most effective evaluation devices of bibliographic instruction are provided by Paul Cappuzzello from OCLC, Janet Freedman from Southeastern Massachusetts University and James Warrington, Jr. from Earlham College.

Kirkendall, Carolyn. "Library Instruction: A Column of Opinion." *Journal of Academic Librarianship* 7 (September, 1981): 236–237.

This column sought reactions to the statement that the complexities of libraries and the lack of knowledgeable library staff is not a rationale for user instruction but for more library staff education. Mary Dolven from Diablo Valley College, Suzy Turner from Mississippi State University, Ron Martin from Kansas State University, Vivian Wood from Rutgers University and Sandra Yee from Muskegon Community College provided responses.

Kirkendall, Carolyn. "Library Instruction. A Column of Opinion." *Journal of Academic Librarianship* 7 (November, 1981): 292–293.

This column discusses three reasons for bibliographic instruction: 1) It is good for people to know how to use libraries; 2) libraries are made unnecessarily difficult for users; 3) librarians want to improve their image by becoming teachers. Reactions to these reasons are given by Judy Reynolds from San Jose State University, Judy Avery from the University of Michigan, and David Carlson from the University of Evansville.

Kobelski, Pamela and Mary Reichel. "Conceptual Frameworks for Bibliographic Instruction." *Journal of Academic Librarianship* 7 (May 1981): 73–77.

The authors discuss the use of seven conceptual frameworks

to organize the content of bibliographic instruction. Included is a discussion of cognitive learning theory which outlines the importance of conceptual frameworks in teaching students bibliographic information.

Kozak, Karen. *Goals of the Eighties.* Proceedings from the 1981 Spring Meeting of the Nebraska Library Association, College and University Section. ERIC Document Reproduction Service, 1981. ED 207 548.

Included are eight papers on various apsects of librarianship to stimulate growth and activity. Several papers deal with library instruction such as users' guides and videotapes as an aid in library instruction.

Langer, Monica. "Academic Libraries: Fetishism of Information or Centre of Education." *Canadian Library Journal* 38 (February, 1981): 25–28.

Argues that academic librarians should become more involved in the educational activities within their academic institutions.

Lee, Joann H. and Arthur H. Miller, Jr. "Introducing Online Data Base Searching in the Small Academic Library: A Model for Service Without Charge to Undergraduates." *Journal of Academic Librarianship* 7 (March, 1981): 14–22.

Describes the two-year experience with on-line database searching in the Lake Forest College Library which serves 1,000 students and 100 faculty. On-line database searching is part of the reference service and used in conjunction with bibliographic instruction. Objectives, planning and implementation are discussed in detail. Information on equipment, vendors, personnel and clientele is provided. The authors describe search strategy and interview techniques for on-line database searching and give some brief facts about evaluation.

Lester, Linda and others. *Committee on Library Orientation Report to the Director's Council: Library Sign Systems.* ERIC Document Reproduction Service, 1980. ED 196 452.

Reviews the need for a unified, well-designed sign system at the University of Virginia library to help orient the users.

Library Skills Course for EOP Students. ERIC Document Reproduction Service, 1981. ED 202 459.

Describes a five-week library skills course at Plattsburg State University College for Educational Opportunity Program (EOP) students. Worksheets and an evaluation questionnaire are included.

Lubans, John, Jr. "Library Literacy." *RQ* 21 (Winter, 1981): 121–123.

This column, written by Richard A Dreifuss, addresses library instruction and graduate students. Points out that graduate instructors feel graduate students should have obtained library skills during their undergraduate years or earlier. Librarians may be able to work with graduate students to help convince graduate instructors of the need for library instruction to these students.

Malley, Ian. "Aspects of User Education in U.K. Academic Libraries, 1976–1981." *Education Libraries Bulletin* 24 (1981): 1–15.

Martin, Jess A. and others. "PLATO in the Library." *Southeastern Librarian* (Spring, 1981): 14–15.

PLATO, a computer-assisted instruction system, is used for orientation and instruction in the library at the University of Tennessee Center for the Health Sciences. This program is described and evaluated.

McNemar, Donald W. *The Researcher and the Librarian.* ERIC Document Reproduction Service, 1981. ED 195 279.

Advocates a closer partnership between academic librarians and researchers through a more active leadership on the part of librarians.

Merrill, Martha. "Another Opinion About Library Instruction." *Southeastern Librarian* (Summer, 1981): 70–71.

This is a reaction to accusing librarians of teaching students to be librarians. The author feels it is necessary to teach students in this way so they can become self-sufficient in libraries.

Mitchell, Marguerite. "The Library Skills Workbook at Stephens College." *Show-Me Libraries* 32 (January, 1981): 32–33.

Molendyke, Joseph A. "Assessing the Efficiency of Library Orientation in the Regional Campus System." *Technological Horizons in Education* 8 (March, 1981): 52–53.

Describes how the use of audiovisual equipment can provide students with orientation to library facilities and services without a physical tour.

Nagy, Laslo A. and Martha L. Thomas. "An Evaluation of the Teaching Effectiveness of Two Library Instructional Videotapes." *College and Research Libraries* 42 (January, 1981):

26–30.

Two videotapes on computer database searching and writing a research paper were used with students to teach them library skills. Pre- and post-tests were given to students in a control and experimental group. It was found that students in the experimental group performed better on the post-test than those in the control group.

Newmark, Laura C. *Alternative Search Strategies for Teaching Access to Social Science Research Materials.* ERIC Document Reproduction Service, 1981. ED 196 802.

This study discusses conceptual and bibliographic access to the literature of the social sciences. Examines search strategies, problems of conceptual access to the social science literature and control over terminology. Includes an annotated bibliography of social sciences sources.

"A Non-Credit/Non-Graded Course at the University of Kansas." *College and Research Libraries News* 42 (June, 1981): 173–174.

Librarians at the University of Kansas at Lawrence have developed a non-credit/non-graded course for basic research skills described here. This seven-week course seems to be a successful venture at a medium-sized university with an enrollment of 23,000 students.

Oberman-Soroka, Cerise. *Petals Around a Rose: Abstract Reasoning and Bibliographic Instruction.* Chicago: ALA, ACRL, 1980.

This paper was presented as part of the ALA ACRL Bibliographic Instruction Section program at the Annual Conference in New York, July 1, 1980 entitled "Learning Theory in Action: Applications in Bibliographic Instruction." It discusses bibliographic instruction from the point of view of abstract reasoning as theorized by Jean Piaget. The author discusses a library skills credit course which she taught for undergraduates at the College of Charleston. She organizes her course around three basic components: analysis, linkage and evaluation. The appendix includes guided design for collective problem solving.

Pagel, Scott B. "Bibliographic Instruction in the Humanities." In *Library Problems in the Humanities* edited by Thomas P. Slavens. New York: K.G. Saur, 1981. p31–34.

Pausch, Lois and Jean Koch. "Technical Services Librarians in Library Instruction." *Libri* 31 (September, 1981): 198–204.

Author discusses the use of technical services librarians in library use instruction by giving a number of compelling reasons for this. Summarizes a survey of 300 academic libraries to assess current involvement and levels of participation in library instruction on the part of technical services librarians. One hundred forty libraries responded that they utilized technical services librarians in user instruction. Such involvement seems to be a growing trend in academic libraries.

Pearson, Lennart. "Curriculum — Integrated Library Instruction." *Liberal Education* 66 (Winter, 1980): 402–409.

Person, Roland. "Long-Term Evaluation of Bibliographic Instruction; Lasting Encouragement." *College and Research Libraries* 42 (January, 1981): 19–25.

Reports on a long-term evaluation of the library skills credit course taught at Southern Illinois University at Carbondale. Seven hundred thirty questionnaires were sent to students who had taken this course previously. The questionnaires dealt with biographic data, reactions to the course, open-ended questions about the course and suggestions. Response rate was 25.64 percent. It was found that students found confidence in using the library through the course, have helped other students in using the library and recommend the course to others. They appreciate individualized course related instruction. Students indicated high value for the course.

Pierce, Beverly A. "Librarians and Teachers: Where Is the Common Ground?" *Catholic Library World* 53 (November, 1981): 164–167.

Discusses the problems connected with communication between faculty and academic librarians regarding students' bibliographic skills. Course-related library instruction is advocated.

Pritchard, Eileen. *Library and Classroom Exercises in Science.* ERIC Document Reproduction Service, 1980. ED 188 910.

Gives ten exercises for students in biology to teach them the use of the literature in science, technology and agriculture.

Quantic, Diane D. *Developing a Cooperative Library Skills Program.* ERIC Document Production Service, 1981. ED 206 001.

Advocates developing a college library instruction program through joint efforts of the faculty and librarians. Provides objectives for such a program. Problem-solving skills should be emphasized.

Quiring, Virginia and others. *Academic Library Instruction in Kansas. A Directory*. ERIC Document Reproduction Service, 1981. ED 206 308.

The directory is based on a 1980 survey of 36 academic libraries in Kansas and summarizes their bibliographic instruction activities.

Rader, Hannelore B. "Bibliographic Instruction. Second International Conference on User Education." *College and Research Library News* 42 (November, 1981): 359.

Summarizes the program of the Second International Conference on User Education in Oxford, England, July 7–10, 1981.

Rice, James, Jr. *Teaching Library Use. A Guide for Library Instruction*. Westport, CT: Greenwood Press, 1981.

The objective of this work is to aid librarians and teachers in designing library instruction programs on any level. It can also be used as a textbook for courses on library instruction. Included are sections on planning, library orientation, instruction, testing and evaluation, signage and instructional materials. A number of appendices offer supplementary materials.

Rothstein, Pauline. *The Development of a Model and Curriculum Design in Information Utilization for Education Students*. Ph.D. Dissertation, Fordham University, 1981. DAI, vol. 41 A, p4598. Also available in the ERIC system ED 190 543.

The investigator tried to develop a model to train education students with different information needs under diverse circumstances in information utilization skills using the Training System Model (TSM). A module on the awareness of materials and services was fully developed including a training manual and evaluation instruments. This was tested on four graduate students in education and case studies were developed. Further research for four additional modules in the TSM are needed.

Sayles, Jeremy. "A Response." *Southeastern Librarian* (Summer, 1981): 73–74.

Author provides a response to M. Merrill and G. Vickery's comments on his earlier article accusing librarians teaching students to be librarians. He continues to be critical of the library instruction movement's "over-emphasis" on teaching students the complicated dynamics of information retrieval.

Schwartz, Barbara A. and Susan Burton. *Teaching Library Skills in Freshman English: An Undergraduate Library's Experience*.

Austin, Texas: University of Texas at Austin, General Libraries, 1981.

This publication describes in detail the course-integrated library instruction program for freshman English at the University of Texas Undergraduate Library. Five thousand students are taught library skills each year through this program. Positive and negative aspects of this five-year-old program are discussed. Included is information on resource needs, staff capabilities, faculty-library cooperation, objectives, and instructional materials.

Shrigley, Roger. "Reader Education." *New Library World* 82 (March, 1981): 42–43.

Author reports his academic library's user instruction program which evolved from the need of having to provide reader instruction to 1,600 students in 20 subject areas. Also discussed is the "overkill" effort of instruction librarians who may be providing too much instruction. Author feels the one-to-one reader instruction is most effective but should be used creatively.

Silverman, Sharon and others. "Ideas in Practice: Where's the Periodical Guide to Books? Or Library Instruction in Developmental Education." *Journal of Developmental and Remedial Education* 4 (Spring, 1981): 16–17.

Describes and assesses a library skills instruction unit offered at Kendall College in Illinois to students in a course on basic writing and library use.

Skinner, Jane and Judith Violette. *A Directory of Library Instruction Programs in Indiana Academic Libraries.* ERIC Document Reproduction Service, 1981. ED 191 487.

Reports results of a survey of 40 academic libraries in Indiana and summarizes their library use instruction program.

Smalley, Topsy N. *Basic Reference Tools for Nursing Research. A Workbook with Explanations and Examples.* ERIC Document Reproduction Service, 1981. ED 197 071.

This is a workbook for nursing students to teach them literature searching skills in medicine, nursing and allied health. Exercises are included.

Stebelman, Scott. *Evaluation of Self-Paced Library Instruction at the University of Nebraska – Lincoln Libraries.* ERIC Document Reproduction Service, 1981. ED 197 742.

Findings indicate that self-paced library instruction is a viable alternative for library orientation tours, computer-assisted instruction and tutorials. Included is a library skills test as well as a demographic and attitudinal questionnaire.

Stewart, Frances. "Teaching Library Usage Through Programmed Instruction at Alabama A & M University." *The Alabama Librarian* 32 (November-December, 1980): 8–11.
    Offers rationale for a course on library instruction at Alabama A & M University, gives some definitions of library instruction terms, goals and objectives for the course and methods of instruction.

Stoffle, Carla J. "The Library's Role in Facilitating Quality Teaching." *New Directions for Teaching and Learning* 5 (1981): 67–78.
    Discusses how librarians in academic institutions can become involved in the teaching/learning process on campus through teaching students library skills in collaboration with faculty. Programs at Earlham College and the University of Wisconsin-Parkside are presented as examples.

Stoffle, Carla J. and others. "A Workbook Approach to Teaching Library Research Skills." *Urban Academic Librarian* 1 (Spring, 1981): 19–24.
    Describes the advantages and disadvantages of using workbooks for teaching basic and advanced library skills based on the University of Wisconsin-Parkside experience. Also discusses the development of the workbooks and the reaction of students and faculty toward the use of the workbooks.

Walker, Linda K. "The Texas Collection and the Freshman Research Paper." *Texas Libraries* 43 (Fall, 1981): 108–112.
    Author, who is an English instructor at Baylor University, shows how freshmen can be made to realize the value of the information in libraries through library instruction.

White, Donald J. "Workbook for Basic Library Instruction." *Canadian Library Journal* 38 (August, 1981): 213–219.
    Discusses advantages of using workbooks in basic library instruction for undergraduates. Compares the use of workbooks with effectiveness of AV instruction, group instruction, lectures, and tours.

Whitmore, Marilyn P. *Instructing the Academic Library User in the United States and Britain: A Review of the Literature and the State-of-Art in Oxford.* ERIC Document Reproduction Service,

144

1981. ED 207 599.

Discusses the various approaches to library instruction used in the U.S. and Britain based on 60 citations.

Wilbert, Shirley. "Library Pathfinders Come Alive." *Journal of Education for Librarianship* 21 (Spring, 1981): 345–349.

Discusses the use of pathfinders to help users gain access to the abundance of information available in libraries. Gives history of pathfinder development and describes their use at the University of Wisconsin – Oshkosh, where undergraduates in a library science course are required to create pathfinders. Their use and cost are also described.

Williams, Nyal Z. and Jack T. Tsukamoto. *Library Instruction and Faculty Development. Growth Opportunities in the Academic Community*. Ann Arbor, MI: Pierian Press, 1980.

These are the papers presented at the 23rd Midwest Academic Librarians' Conference held at Ball State University, May, 1978. They include an article on faculty development by Jesse M. Cartney, Dwight F. Burlingame, Paul H. Lacey, and William K. Stephenson. Patricia S. Breivik discusses library instruction and instructional development, Evan I. Farber talks about the course-related library instruction at Earlham College and a panel provides a critique of the faculty development and library instruction movement.

Wolf, Carolyn E. and Richard Wolf. *Basic Library Skills, a Short Course*. Jefferson, NC: McFarland and Co., Inc., 1981.

This is a short textbook to be used as a self-paced instructional manual for courses which teach the use of the library. Performance objectives are stated at the beginning of each of the 12 chapters. Exercises, important terms and a list of sources are given at the end of each chapter. The appendix includes answers to the exercises. The chapters cover a walking tour of the library, the card catalog, bibliographies, book reviews, dictionaries, directories, periodicals, literary criticisms, government documents, biographies, business and consumer information, non-print materials and special hints for researching papers.

Worley, Joan H. "Bibliographic Instruction. Bibliographic Competencies for Education Students." *College and Research Library News* 42 (July-August, 1981): 209–210.

The ACRL Education and Behavioral Sciences Section Bibliographic Instruction for Educators Committee developed guidelines for bibliographic competencies for education students which are described in this report.

Young, Arthur P. "And Gladly Teach: Bibliographic Instruction and the Library." *Advances in Librarianship* 10. Edited by Michael Harris. New York: Academic Press, 1980, p63–88.

Discusses the status of bibliographic instruction in academic and school libraries through a review of the literature and by giving specific examples of research studies. Discusses rationale, the educational environment, evaluation and instructional patterns.

PUBLIC LIBRARIES

Lubans, John, Jr. "Library Literacy." *RQ* 20 (Summer, 1981): 337–339.

This column focuses on the public library and user education and provides several reasons for instruction in public library use.

Thwaits, Margaret B. *Academic Library Instruction Program for Developmentally Disabled Adults.* ERIC Document Reproduction Service, 1981. ED 205 220.

This library instruction program for developmentally disabled adults was developed at Colorado State University and was taught in combination with a course on reading skills. Pre- and post-tests, learning activities, and an assessment of this course are included. It is suggested that this course is more appropriately taught in a public library.

Wilson, T.D. *Guidelines for Developing and Implementing a National Plan for Training and Education in Information Use.* ERIC Document Reproduction Service, 1981. ED 201 336.

Suggests national policies on user training can be related to national information policies. Gives lines of action for a national policy of user training. Provides a systematic plan to implement and evaluate such guidelines.

SCHOOL LIBRARIES

Biddle, Michaelle L. "Planning and Design of the High School Library Use Instruction Program." *Catholic Library World* 53 (November, 1981): 160–163.

High school librarians can provide library use education to most of the future adult population. This article stresses the importance of well-defined plans for user instruction, interaction with teachers, cooperation with teachers to define the users' information needs, setting behavioral objectives and revising the instruction plans as needed.

Doyen, Salley E. "A Study of Library Skills Instruction." *Top of the News* 38 (Fall, 1981): 60–63.

The Elementary Library Media Skills Curriculum. Grades K–6. ERIC Document Reproduction Service, 1981. ED 205 199.
This is a New York State curriculum guide developed to integrate library skills into the curriculum of K–6 levels. Appendix includes library media vocabulary for students, list of schools which are participating in the field testing of this guide and a bibliography.

George, Bette L. *The Effectiveness of Self-Paced Instruction in Teaching Reference Skills to Heterogeneously-Grouped Elementary School Students.* ERIC Document Reproduction Service, 1981. ED 206 283.
This study includes an extensive search of the literature to identify promising methods of teaching library skills to elementary school students. Includes a pilot project to test the methods identified as to their effectiveness. Appendices include testing materials, instructional materials and 31 citations.

Gratch, Bonnie. "Research Can Lead to Change." *School Library Journal* 28 (December 1981): 35.

Hoagland, Sister Mary K. "Library Skills – Caught or Taught?" *Catholic Library World* 53 (November, 1981): 173–175.
Describes the library skills program throughout the Archdiocese of the Philadelphia School System using volunteers and librarians.

Irving, Ann. "Some Impressions of Library User Education in U.S. Schools: Report of the Visit in May, 1981." *British Library Research and Development Report* No. 5652. London: British Library, 1981.

Johnson, Kerry A. "Instructional Development in Schools: A Proposed Model." *School Media Quarterly* 9 (Summer, 1981): 256–260, 269–271.
Author discusses the school media specialist's role in the curriculum development. Provides a model for the school instructional design based on the involvement of the school library media specialist.

Kelner, Bernard G. and Joan B. Myers. *Key Competencies. Libraries. Elementary, Junior High and Senior High*. ERIC Document Reproduction Service, 1981. ED 192 780.

Identifies essential library skills for students in grades K–12 in the Philadelphia school district. Provides profile for each grade.

"Librarians and English Teachers. Part II." *English Journal* 70 (November, 1981): 75–77.

This section continues comments by high school librarians on how fully they can best cooperate with the English teachers in providing students with knowledge of books and library skills. (See also "Our Readers Write . . . .")

Marland, Michael. *Information Skills in the Secondary Curriculum: The Recommendations of a Working Group Sponsored by the British Library and the Schools Council*. London: Methuen Education for the Schools Council, 1981.

This booklet focuses on the assignment or project work method of teaching in secondary education as the vehicle for the teaching of information skills. A special curriculum which teaches library skills every year on a more advanced level is advocated.

Molloy, Wendy and others. "Innovations and Practice: Competence with Independence." *Australian Journal of Reading* 4 (August, 1981): 149–152.

Discusses a program of language arts skills for students in grades 5–7. Included among others are critical thinking and library skills to train students toward independent use of these skills.

Moskowitz, Michael A. "High School Libraries: How to Introduce Thirty Sophomore Classes to Their High School Libraries and Have Them Come Back for More." *Clearing House* 54 (May, 1981): 418–422.

Describes a two-day library instruction program for all sophomore English classes at Quincy High and Vocational Technical schools in Massachusetts. Instruction is geared to class needs through the use of computer-scored pre-tests.

"Our Readers Write. What Would Librarians and English Teachers Most Like to Say to Each Other?" *English Journal* 70 (April, 1981): 60–66.

High school English teachers and librarians comment on how

they can cooperate to provide students with the best English curriculum and library skills.

Povsic, Frances F. *Teaching Media Skills: Selected Sources.* ERIC Document Reproduction Service, 1980. ED 200 213.
This is a bibliography of materials to facilitate the teaching of library skills in K–12.

Sayer, David E. "Towards Individuality: The School Library." *School Librarian* 29 (March, 1981): 216–220.

Trigg, Stanley. "The Use of the Library." *The School Librarian* 29 (December, 1981): 302–306.
Discusses the use of work sheets in teaching library skills to elementary and secondary school students. Describes location and evaluation skills to be taught to pupils.

Turk, Beatrice. "Tradition! Tradition! Or Using Media to Teach Media Center Skills." *Ohio Media Spectrum* 33 (July, 1981): 12–16.
Author discusses a media skills program for eighth graders using the students themselves in producing a play on video cassette to teach these skills.

SPECIAL LIBRARIES

Davies, D.T. "Case Studies and Simulation Exercises in Engineering User Education at Lancaster Polytechnic." *ISG News* 18/19 (August/December, 1981): 4–8.

Marcotte, Joan M. and K.J. Graves. "Library Instruction Within the Medical Record Administration Curriculum." *Bulletin of the Medical Library Association* 69 (1981): 240–246.
The University of Tennessee Center for the Health Sciences Library has developed a course for medical record administration (MRA) students, which is described in this article. The objectives of this course are met by integrating library use instruction in the MRA curriculum. Teaching methods and evaluation techniques used in this course are applicable to library instruction in other disciplines.

Merrick, Nancy P. and Robert M. Braude. "Computer-Assisted Instruction in a Health Sciences Library: An Experimental Project." *Bulletin of the Medical Library Association* 69 (January, 1981): 21–25.

Using grant funds the University of Nebraska Library of Medicine studied management aspects of providing computer-assisted instruction to faculty and students. A survey of users, the methodology for implementing the pilot project, and the future of CAI at the University of Nebraska are described.

Shearer, Barbara and others. *Bibliographic Instruction Through the Related Studies Division in Vocational Education: LRC Guide, Pathfinders, and Script for Slide Presentation.* ERIC Document Reproduction Service, 1981. ED 205 171.

Describes the library instruction course offered by the Learning Resource Center at Tennessee's Tri-Cities State Technical Institute. Provides an outline, pathfinders for technical subjects, a guide to LRC, an evaluation questionnaire and a script for an instructional slide presentation.

Singer, Carol A. *Doing Research with U.S. Government Documents in the United States Conn Library.* ERIC Document Reproduction Services, 1981. ED 197 756.

This is a guide for library users trying to do research using government documents in a depository collection. A worksheet format is utilized.

Stieg, Margaret F. "The Information Needs of Historians." *College and Research Libraries* (November, 1981): 549–560.

This summarizes the results of a survey of historians in different fields of history. Included is information on how historians obtain their information, relevant references and how they use materials in other languages. Comparisons with other surveys in this area are provided.

Streatfield, D.R. and others. "Assessment of an Illuminative Evaluation Programme for Information Services." *Aslib Proceedings* 33 (February, 1981): 67–70.

Article describes the use of illuminative evaluation in assessing the innovative project concerned with information gathering in social services departments.

Streatfield, D.R. and others. "A Problem-Based Training Approach to Information for Practitioners." *Libri* 31 (September, 1981): 243–257.

Describes a user education program at the University of Sheffield in England to help social services personnel satisfy their information needs. Outlines scientific information service model and a library custodial model. Courses for social services information users are described.

ALL LEVELS

Bafundo, Donna R. *In-Service Training Program for Library Para-professionals: A Report.* ERIC Document Reproduction Service, 1981. ED 207 536.

This is the final report of an in-service training program for paraprofessionals in libraries sponsored by the Virginia State Library and designed by an area library networking committee. Included among other modules was a 10-week course on library skills.

Berry, John. "Pilgrim's Progress and the Bible." *Library Journal* 106 (April 15, 1981): 831.

This editorial discusses the national crisis in library use instruction. Much of the problem with library illiteracy seems to stem from the fact that schools are not doing their job in teaching library skills. A national library skills program is advocated.

Dickinson, Dennis W. "Library Literacy: Who? When? Where?" *Library Journal* 106 (April 15, 1981): 853–855.

Discusses the inadequacy of library skills programs in elementary and secondary schools and shows how this has created problems for academic librarians. Advocates that school librarians become more involved in providing library skills instruction to students.

Ellison, John W. "Media Librarianship. Effective Library Instruction and the Learning Process." *Catholic Library World* 53 (November, 1981): 182–184.

Author examines factors which influence learning in order to provide improved library skills instruction. Motivation, physical and intellectual ability, meaningful results, knowledge of results and social growth are important factors to consider when planning bibliographic instruction.

Fox, Peter. *Second International Conference on Library User Education. Proceedings.* Loughborough: INFUSE Publications, 1981.

These are the papers presented at the Second Instruction Conference on Library User Education at Keble College, Oxford from July 7–10, 1981. Included are Constance Mulligan's "Speaking in Tongues: Erecting a Professional Tower of Babel;" Dai Haunsell's "Teaching and Learning Information Skills: A Sense of Purpose;" James E. Herring's "The Politics of User

Education in Schools;" Terry Brake's "User Education Is Dead: Long Live Education;" Ed Marman's "Design and Development of a Pre-School to Adult Library Instruction Curriculum in the Wayne-Westland (Michigan) Community School District;" Robert Pearce's "The Overseas Student and Library Use: A Special Case for Treatment;" D.R. Streatfield's and T.D. Wilson's "A Problem-Based Approach to User Education: Recent Experience in Social Services Departments;" Ron Scrivener's "User Education in Public Libraries: A Practical Exercise;" Hannelore B. Rader's "Insuring User Instruction in Academic Libraries Through Involvement in Curriculum Development;" David Jones' "Team Teaching in User Education;" John Lubans Jr.'s "Evaluation Design: Some Methodological Observations and Suggestions;" Rao Aluri's and Mary Reichel's "Evaluation of Student Learning in Library-Use: Instructional Programmes Based on Cognitive Learning Theory;" John James' and David Fulljames' "A Longitudinal Study of the Interactions of Science Students with the Polytechnic Library;" Patrick Condon's "User Education in Australia;" Gulein Cribb's "User Education in a Developing Country: Turkey;" Deborah Masters' "User Education to New Technology: The Experience of U.S. Academic Libraries;" and Graham Gibbs' "Putting It All into Practice." A final summary by Peter Taylor puts the whole conference into perspective.

Hodges, Gerald G. "Library-Use Instruction: The Librarian's Challenge and Responsibility." *Catholic Library World* 53 (November, 1981): 176–179.
    This article focuses on methods for developing library instruction programs on all levels, the identification of appropriate instructional strategies and continuing education for instructional libraries. The article includes a table on competencies for library skills K–12 and one for library orientation in academic libraries.

"Instruction in Library User." In *Reference Services* edited by D.E. Davinson. New York: K.G. Saur, 1980. p175–206.

Lubans, John, Jr. "Library Literacy." *RQ* 20 (Spring, 1981): 233–235.
    Jon Lindgren from Lawrence University discusses library literacy in detail in this column. He uses library literacy to define user instruction as a specific educational skill as well as being central to the goals of education.

152

McClure, Charles R. *Chickasha Cooperative Bibliographic Instruction Project: Final Evaluation*. ERIC Document Reproduction Service, 1981. ED 203 860.

Describes a cooperative bibliographic instruction project between a public university and high school library to teach library skills to high school students, college students and other library users. Included are objectives, evaluations, instructional methods and ten recommendations. Appendix includes various collected data, a workbook, publicity and slide-tape scripts.

Pastine, Maureen and Karen Seibert. "Update on the Status of Bibliographic Instruction in Library School Programs." *Journal of Education for Librarianship* 21 (Fall, 1980): 169–171.

Summarizes the answers to a survey of the 67 ALA and 33 AALS library school programs. The responses indicate that the status of bibliographic instruction has not improved substantially since earlier surveys reported in 1976 and 1978.

Reynolds, Linda and Stephen Barrett. *Signs and Guiding for Libraries*. London: Bingley, 1981.

This book, written with the support of the British Library Research and Development Department, gives practical advice on the production of coordinated and pleasing systems of graphics for libraries. Discussed are sign production, design principles, principles of sign design and others.

Ridgeway, Patricia M. "ALA Approves Instruction Policy/Orientation Round-Up." *South Carolina Librarian* 25 (Fall, 1981): 12.

Gives the policy statement in regards to library use instruction adopted by the ALA Committee on Instruction in Use of Libraries.

Ridgeway, Patricia M. "Coordination of Bibliographic Instruction Programs/Instruction Round-Up." *South Carolina Librarian* 25 (Spring, 1981): 9–10, 28.

Discusses the lack of communication between academic and school librarians as related to library instruction in South Carolina. Summarizes the symposium which addressed this cooperation in January, 1981 at Meredith College in North Carolina.

Schmidt, Janine. "Reader Education in the Eighties." *Australian Library Journal* 30 (August, 1981): 97–104.

This paper reviews reader education, its history, present status and future possibilities. Author tries to provide summaries of the status of reader education in the United States, the United

Kingdom and Australia.

Shapiro, Lillian L. "Comment on Library Instruction: A Difficult Dilemma." *Catholic Library World* 53 (November, 1981): 185–188.

The author comments on the why, what, how and where of library instruction. Other librarians also provide comments on L. Shapiro's comments.

Vickery, George W. "More Opinions About Library Instruction." *Southeastern Librarian* (Summer, 1981): 71–72.

This discusses what may be appropriate service in terms of the reference transaction relating to user instruction. The eternal reference dilemma of whether to give the specific information to the user or whether to instruct the user to find the information alone is addressed.

TWELFTH ANNUAL LIBRARY INSTRUCTION CONFERENCE:

PARTICIPANTS

May 6 & 7, 1982

Sponsored by the LOEX Clearinghouse and the
Division of Continuing Education
Eastern Michigan University

Carl L. Adams
  Audiovisual Librarian
College of St. Francis
Joliet, IL 60435

Rao Aluri
  Assistant Professor
Div. of Libr. & Inf. Management
Emory University
Atlanta, GA 30322

Thomas V. Atkins
  Chair — Library Inst. Services
Baruch College
New York, NY 10010

Judith C. Avery
  Instruction Librarian
Undergraduate Library
University of Michigan
Ann Arbor, MI 48109

Shaleen Barnes
  Instruction Librarian
Southeastern Massachusetts Univ.
N. Dartmouth, MA 02747

Steven V. Baumeister
  Science Librarian
Westminster College
New Wilmington, PA 16142

Dan Bedsole
  Dean of Educational Resources
Austin College
Sherman, TX 75090

Mary E. Bell
  Reference Librarian
Pattee Library
Pennsylvania State University
University Park, PA 16802

Patricia A. Berge
  Coord.: Reference Services
University of Wisconsin–Parkside
Kenosha, WI 53141

James A. Belz
  Ref/BI Coordinator
Univ. of Wisconsin–Milwaukee
Milwaukee, WI 53201

Judith Blaford
  Libn/Media Specialist
University of Illinois
Urbana, IL 61801

G. Elaine Blowers
  Undergraduate Services
Northern Illinois University
DeKalb, IL 60115

155

Marilyn G. Bodnar
  Reference Librarian
Lycoming College
Williamsport, PA 17701

Dorita Bolger
  Reference Librarian
McGill Library
Westminster College
New Wilmington, PA 16142

Morell D. Boone
  Director
Center of Educational Resources
Eastern Michigan University
Ypsilanti, MI 48197

Terrence Brake
  Director--Information Skills in
  the Curriculum Research Unit
Inner London Education Auth.
Centre for Learning Resources
275 Kennington Lane
London SE11 50Z
England

Ellen Brassil
  Coord–User Education
Health Sciences Library
University of North Carolina
Chapel Hill, NC 27514

Barbara A. Brock
  Librarian/Instructor
Carlson Library
University of Toledo
Toledo, OH 43606

Mary E. Brennan
  Reference Librarian
Fackenthal Library
Franklin & Marshall College
Lancaster, PA 17603

Leah H. Brown
  Reference Librarian
Bailey Library
Slippery Rock State College
Slippery Rock, PA 16057

Gregory Carr
Paley Library
Temple University
Philadelphia, PA 19122

Elena Ester Cevallos
  Ref/Instruction Librarian
Hofstra University
Hempstead, NY 11550

Linda Chemlow
  Reference Librarian
Newman Library
Virginia Polytechnic Institute
  & State University
Blacksburg, VA 24061

Katie Chilton
  Librarian
College of St. Francis Library
600 Taylor St.
Joliet, IL 60435

Marilyn Christianson
  Orientation Librarian
Cunningham Memorial Library
Indiana State University
Terre Haute, IN 47809

Carmen M. Costa de Ramos
  BI Coordinator
Lazaro Memorial Library
University of Puerto Rico
Rio Piedras, PR 00931

Belinda Daniels
  Public Services Librarian

O'Kelly Library
Winston-Salem State University
Winston-Salem, NC 27110

Doris Dantin
  Orientation/Instruction Coord.
Middleton Library
Louisiana State University
Baton Rouge, LA 70803

Lyn Davidge
  Assoc. Reference Librarian
Hatcher Graduate Library
University of Michigan
Ann Arbor, MI 48109

Willie Mae Dawkins
  Reference/Instruction Librarian
University of Wisconsin—Parkside
Kenosha, WI 53141

Betty H. Day
  Reference Librarian
Hornbake Library
University of Maryland
College Park, MD 20742

Linda DiSante
Beaver Campus Library
Pennsylvania State University
Brodhead Road
Monaca, PA 15061

Maria Dittman
  Reference/Instruction/Librarian
Memorial Library
Marquette University
Milwaukee, WI 53235

Gay Dixon
  Head: Reference Department
Strozier Library
Florida State University
Tallahassee, FL 32303

Sasha Dow
  Assistant Librarian
Taubman Medical Library
University of Michigan
Ann Arbor, MI 48109

Rheba Dupras
  Reader Services Librarian
Rasmuson Library
University of Alaska
Fairbanks, Alaska 99701

Susan Eichelberger
  BI Coordinator
Cullom-Davis Library
Bradley University
Peoria, IL 61625

Mary Jane Engh
  BI Librarian
Owen Science/Engineering
  Library
Washington State University
Pullman, WA 99163

Jill Fatzer
  Head: Reference Department
University of Delaware
Newark, DE 19711

Gloria Freimer
  Instructor/Librarian
Carlson Library
University of Toledo
Toledo, OH 43606

Kathy Fulton
  Reference Librarian
Hogue LRC
Bee County College
Beeville, TX 78102

Nancy Garner
  Reference/Documents Librarian

Curry Library
William Jewell College
Liberty, MO 64068

Mary W. George
  Head: General Reference
Firestone Library
Princeton University
Princeton, NJ 08544

Mary Joan Gleason
  Faculty Services Librarian
Wilmot Library
Nazareth College of Rochester
Rochester, NY 14610

Julia Chance Gustafson
  Reference Librarian
Andrews Library
College of Wooster
Wooster, OH 44691

Linda Guyotte
  Assistant Librarian
Mann Library
Cornell University
Ithaca, NY 14850

Voanne Hansen
  Reference Librarian
Kirkwood Community Coll. LRC
Cedar Rapids, IA 52406

Larry Hardesty
  Head: Reference Department
West Library
DePauw University
Greencastle, IN 46135

Lynn Harper
  Asst. Reference Librarian
Memorial Library
James Madison University
Harrisonburg, VA 22801

Mary Ellen Hegedus
  Public Services Librarian
Fritz Library
University of North Dakota
Grand Forks, ND 58202

Luella Hemingway
  BI Coordinator
Emory University
Atlanta, GA 30322

Sharon Ann Hogan
  Deputy Director
Temple University Libraries
Philadephia, PA 19122

Doris K. Hosler
  Ganser Library
Millersville,State College
Millersville, PA 17551

Evelyn Hui
  Graphic/Photo Specialist
University of Wisconsin--Parkside
  Library
Kenosha, WI 53141

Carleton Jackson
  Coord:'Library Instruction
Hornbake Undergraduate Library
University of Maryland
College Park, MD 20742

Kathleen Jenkins
  Coord: Library Instruction
Booth Library
Eastern Illinois University
Charleston, IL 61920

Tim Jewell
  Head: Reference Dept.
Bowling Green State University
Bowling Green, OH 43403

Shirley M. Johnson
  Head: Circulation; Asst. Ref.
Hamilton College Library
Clinton, NY 13323

Dan Joldersma
  Director
Mossey LRC
Hillsdale College
Hillsdale, MI 49242

Linda Katzoff-Grodofsky
  Ref./Collection Development
Paley Library
Temple University
Philadelphia, PA 18122

Faith D. Kindness
  Reference Librarian
Case Library
Colgate University
Hamilton, NY 13346

David King
  Coord: User Education
Texas Medical Center Library
Houston Academy of Medicine
Houston, TX 77135

Carolyn Kirkendall
  Director
LOEX Clearinghouse
Center of Educational Resources
Eastern Michigan University
Ypsilanti, MI 48197

Susan C. Klein
  Instruction Librarian
Murphy Library
University of Wisconsin–LaCrosse
La Crosse, WI 54601

Nancy M. Kline
  Head: Instructional Services
Library

University of Connecticut
Storrs, CT 06268

Bonnie Knauss
  Ref. Libn./Special Collections
Curry Library
William Jewell College
Liberty, MO 64068

Douglas Koschik
  Librarian
Delta College
University Center, MI 48710

John Kupersmith
  Asst. for Public Services
  Programs
General Libraries, PCL 3.200
University of Texas--Austin
Austin, TX 78712

Ross T. LaBaugh
  Assoc. Libn.: Instruction
Southeastern Massachusetts Univ.
N. Dartmouth, MA 02747

Claire Laburn
  Library Instruction Librarian
Jagger Library
University of Cape Town
Rondebosch 7700
South Africa

Berkeley Laite
  Reference Librarian
Lehman Memorial Library
Shippensburg State College
Shippensburg, PA 17257

Carol Laite
  Reference Librarian
Shippensburg State College
Shippensburg, PA 17257

Wilma Lampman
  Reference Librarian
Morris Library
Southern Illinois University
Carbondale, IL 62901

Joann H. Lee
  Head: Reader Services
Lake Forest College Library
Lake Forest, IL 60045

Maxine Leeds
  Reference Librarian
Loyola University
New Orleans, LA 70118

M.L. Leget
  Reference Librarian
Weeks Library
University of South Dakota
Vermillion, SD 57069

Joel Leonard
  Reference Librarian
California State University
Chico, CA 95929

Megan Lilly
  User Education Librarian
Chisholm Institute of Technology
Caulfield East, Victoria 3145
Australia

Jon Lindgren
  Head: Reference Department
Owen D. Young Library
St. Lawrence University
Canton, NY 13617

Tom McNally
  Reference Librarian
Sullivant Hall Undergrad. Lib.
Ohio State University
Columbus, OH 43210

Rebecca Mazur
  Reference Librarian
Fenwick Library
George Mason University
Fairfax, VA 22030

Gerry Meek
  Orientation Librarian
University of Waterloo
Waterloo
Ontario N2L 3G1
Canada

Constance A. Mellon
  Coord: Library Instruction
Univ. of Tennessee--Chattanooga
Chattanooga, TN 37402

Laurel Minott
  Assistant Documents Librarian
Univ. of Illinois--Chicago Circle
Chicago, IL 60640

Stella F. Mosborg
  Assoc. Residence Halls Librarian
University of Illinois
204 E. Peabody Drive
Champaign, IL 61820

Constance P. Mulligan
  Coord: Instructional Services
Northern Kentucky University
Highland Heights, KY 41076

David J. Norden
  Head: Undergraduate Library
University of Michigan
Ann Arbor, MI 48109

Cerise Oberman
  Head: Reference Services
Walter Library
University of Minnesota
Minneapolis, MN 55455

Molly O'Hara
  Assistant Reference Librarian
Univ. of Illinois--Chicago Circle
Chicago, IL 60680

Laura Olson
  Reference Librarian
Smith Library
Hobart & William Smith Colleges
Geneva, NY 14456

Kathryn Owens
  Orientation Librarian
Cunningham Memorial Library
Indiana State University
Terre Haute, IN 47809

Carol B. Penka
  Reference Librarian
University of Illinois
Urbana, IL 61801

Ellen M. Person
  Chair: Library Services Dept.
Lansing Community College
Lansing, MI 48901

Billie Peterson
  Reference Librarian
West Campus LRC
Ohio State University
Columbus, OH 43210

Linda Piele
  Head: Public Services Division
University of Wisconsin--Parkside
Kenosha, WI 53141

Monique Potin
  Faculty Development Officer
University of Montreal
Montreal
Quebec H3C 3J7
Canada

Marcia Preston
  Head: Reference Department
University of Michigan--Dearborn
4901 Evergreen Road
Dearborn, MI 48128

Judith Pryor
  Coordinator of Instruction
University of Wisconsin--Parkside
Kenosha, WI 53141

Hannelore Rader
  Director
University of Wisconsin--Parkside
Library
  Kenosha, WI 53141

Mary Ann Ramey
  Coordinator: BI
Pullen Library
Georgia State University
Atlanta, GA 30324

Daniel Ream
  Reference Librarian
University of Tennessee
Knoxville, TN 37996

Donald Redmond
  Information/Ref. Librarian
Douglas Library
Queen's University
Kingston
Ontario K7L 3K1
Canada

Mary Reichel
  Head: Reference Department
Pullen Library
Georgia State University
Atlanta, GA 30303

Glenn Remelts
  Public Services Librarian

Beloit College
Beloit, WI 53511

Judy Reynolds
  Library Instruction Coord.
San Jose State University
San Jose, CA 95118

Leta B. Ridgeway
  Reference Librarian
Booth Library
Eastern Illinois University
Charleston, IL 61920

Craig Robertson
  Reference/Instruction Libn.
University of Wisconsin–Parkside
Kenosha, WI 53141

Sandra Rosenstock
  Asst. Social Sciences Librarian
Newman Library
Virginia Polytechnic Institute
  & State University
Blacksburg, VA 24061

Roberta Lynne Ruben
  Assistant Prof.–Dept. of Learning
  Resources
Western Illinois University
Macomb, IL 61455

Janell Rudolph
  Reference/Instruction Libn.
Memphis State University
Memphis, TN 38152

Laurie St. Laurent
  Assistant Director
Bensenville Community Public
  Library
Bensenville, IL 60106

Pamela L. Schiffer
  Reference Librarian

Ohio State University
Columbus, OH 43210

Vanette M. Schwartz
  Reference Librarian
Milner Library
Illinois State University
Normal, IL 61761

Jane D. Segal
  User Education Librarian
Ohio State University
Columbus, OH 43210

Judith Sikora
  Reference Librarian
O'Connell Library
Genesee Community College
Batavia, NY 14020

Virginia M. Simpson
  Assistant Librarian
University of Illinois
Urbana, IL 61801

Frederick E. Smith
  Director
Westminster College Library
New Wilmington, PA 16142

Keith Stanger
  Orientation Librarian
Center of Educational Resources
Eastern Michigan University
Ypsilanti, MI 48197

Arena L. Stevens
  Reference Librarian
Indiana University–Northwest
Gary, IN 46408

Barbara E. Stevens
  Director
U.S. Army War College
Carlisle Barracks, PA 17013

Richard Swain
  Reference Librarian
Cleveland State University
Cleveland, OH 44115

R. James Tobin
  Ref. Libn./Instruction Coord.
Bapst Library
Boston College
Chestnut Hill, MA 02167

Richard Tubesing
  Asst. Director: Library Programs
University of Toledo
Toledo, OH 43606

Harold Tuckett
  Reference/Instruction Libn.
University of Wisconsin–Parkside
Kenosha, WI 53141

Charles H. Tunstall
  Instructional/Public Services
  Librarian
Tusculum College
Greeneville, TN 37743

Madelyn Valunas
  Periodicals/Reference Libn.
Shippensburg State College
Shippensburg, PA 17257

Sharon VanDerLaan
  Asst. Reference Librarian
University of Illinois Main Lib.
Urbana, IL 61801

Susan Varca
  BI Coordinator
University of Georgia Library
Athens, GA 30602

Angelo Wallace
  Interim Director, BI Program
Carlson Library

University of Toledo
Toledo, OH 43606

James H. Ward
  Director
Crisman Library
David Lipscomb College
Nashville, TN 37203

Sally Wayman
  Reference Librarian
Pattee Library
Pennsylvania State University
University Park, PA 16802

Guynell Williams
  Asst. Reference Librarian
Donnelley Library
Lake Forest College
Lake Forest, IL 60045

Betsy Wilson
  Asst. Undergraduate Librarian
University of Illinois
Urbana, IL 61801

Betty-Ruth Wilson
  Asst. Undergraduate Librarian
Morris Library
Southern Illinois University
Carbondale, IL 62901

Evelyn H. Winkels
  Reference Librarian
Ireton Library
Marymount College of Virginia
Arlington, VA 22150

Barbara S. Zemanek
  Program Director/Ref. Libn.
Lansing Community College
Lansing, MI 48901